Parents and School Technology

Parents and School Technology

Answers That Reveal Essential Steps for Improvement

Gerard Giordano

ROWMAN & LITTLEFIELD
Lanham • Boulder • New York • London

Published by Rowman & Littlefield
An imprint of The Rowman & Littlefield Publishing Group, Inc.
4501 Forbes Boulevard, Suite 200, Lanham, Maryland 20706
www.rowman.com

Copyright © 2021 Gerard Giordano

All rights reserved. No part of this book may be reproduced in any form or by any electronic or mechanical means, including information storage and retrieval systems, without written permission from the publisher, except by a reviewer who may quote passages in a review.

British Library Cataloguing in Publication Information Available

Library of Congress Cataloging-in-Publication Data On File

ISBN 978-1-4758-5225-7 (cloth)
ISBN 978-1-4758-5226-4 (pbk.)
ISBN 978-1-4758-5227-1 (electronic)

Contents

Preface: Who Has the Right Idea about School Tech?   vii
Acknowledgment   ix

1. Do Computer Experts Have the Right Idea about School Tech?   1
2. Do Angelinos Have the Right Idea about School Tech?   9
3. Do Detroiters Have the Right Idea about School Tech?   17
4. Do Miamians Have the Right Idea about School Tech?   23
5. Do Philadelphians Have the Right Idea about School Tech?   29
6. Do Tampa's Parents Have the Right Idea about School Tech?   35
7. Do Parents in Roselle, Illinois, Have the Right Idea about School Tech?   43
8. Do Silicon Valley's Parents Have the Right Idea about School Tech?   51
9. Do New York City's Parents Have the Right Idea about School Tech?   59
10. Do Salt Lakers Have the Right Idea about School Tech?   67
11. Do San Antonians Have the Right Idea about School Tech?   73
12. Do Seattle's Parents Have the Right Idea about School Tech?   81

References   89
About the Author   125

Preface

Who Has the Right Idea about School Tech?

> [I should have a computer to] have a fair chance at life.
> —Student Myquesha Moore, 2012

> Every child should have a computer.
> —Attorney Lucette Pierre-Louis, 2011

> [Students should have computers to develop the skills they] will need in tomorrow's workforce.
> —Microsoft Corporation, 2017

> [Schools that are] not using [computers] are cheating . . . children.
> —Director Ann Flynn,
> National School Boards Association Technology, 2011

Parents were concerned about problems at their children's schools. They ideally wished to solve them. However, they at least wanted to minimize their impact.

Although parents looked for problems throughout the schools, they were particularly interested in those associated with tech. They had been warned that tech would influence academic achievement, personality traits, and even the careers that their children selected.

The parents easily found problems with tech equipment. They then asked questions about them. For example, they wanted to know why computers were in short supply and high-speed internet was limited.

The parents found problems with tech personnel. They asked why there were so few specially trained teachers and technicians.

The parents wanted to know about tech-related controversies. Some of them had personally experienced them. Others had learned about them from the media. They asked about computer-based testing, eTextbooks, digital content filters, online instruction, student hacking, and spyware.

The parents began by posing their tech questions to teachers. When they were not satisfied with their answers, they went to superintendents and school board members. Some, who still were not satisfied, went to groups outside the schools: they went to businesspeople and elected officials.

This is not the first book to examine school tech. Nonetheless, it is the first to focus on parents. It highlights the problems they detected, the questions they asked, the answers they elicited, the responses they exhibited, and the steps they took.

Although this book stands out because of its content, it also stands out because of its format. It uses intriguing quotes to frame the central issues in each chapter. These quotes come from parents. They also come from the students, teachers, school administrators, businesspeople, politicians, and journalists.

This book stands out for one more important reason: It employs the case method. The case method is an investigative technique that is applied to seemingly unrelated incidents. It then uses probing questions to reveal the complex relationships between those incidents.

This is the second book in a series about the impact that parents have had on schools. The initial volume was *Parents and Textbooks*. This one is *Parents and School Tech*. The next one will be *Parents and School Violence*. All of these books are appropriate for both general and professional audiences.

Acknowledgment

I originally intended this book as a resource for professional educators. However, I changed my mind after my editor, Tom Koerner, suggested that I design it for a general audience. This is one of the countless suggestions that Tom has made and for which I am so indebted to him.

ONE

Do Computer Experts Have the Right Idea about School Tech?

> Parents . . . must insist . . . that [their children get the computer instruction they will need] to succeed in the modern job market.
> —Principal Mashea Ashton, 2018

> I'd rather have my kid . . . on the computer [than in a textbook].
> —Parent Beth Dolobowsky, 2007

> Nine in 10 parents . . . want their child to learn more computer science.
> —Gallup Poll Spokesperson Cynthia English, 2015

> Students without . . . technology . . . feel shame.
> —Journalist George Jones, 2017

Health experts were concerned about the amount of body weight that persons were carrying. They believed that the amount was too high. Tech experts were concerned about computers in the schools. They believed that the number of them was too low. Both groups hoped that public information campaigns would fix these problems. However, they later shifted to shame-inducing campaigns.

FAT SHAMING

Health experts documented that too many Americans were obese. They feared that more would join them.

The experts wished to discourage obesity. However, they doubted that they could do this on their own. They invited the business community to assist them.

Businesspeople were eager to help. They offered weight-loss products. such as public low-calorie foods, appetite-reducing drugs, and exercise equipment.

The businesspeople waited to see how persons would respond to their products. They were excited when many responded enthusiastically.

The health experts were less excited about their partnership with business. They had believed that it would lead to long-term weight reduction. However, they concluded that the reduction was only temporary.

Although the health experts were disappointed, they did not give up. They had another idea. They organized a public information campaign. They used it to showcase the ways in which persons would benefit if they maintained an ideal body weight. They were eager to see its impact.

The experts were again disappointed. They wondered whether they should have designed their campaign differently. They compared it to the federal government's anti-smoking campaign, which had been more effective.

The experts noted that the anti-smoking campaign had informed persons about the danger of smoking and then made them feel ashamed for smoking. They conceded that their own campaign had been much softer.

The health experts resolved to copy the anti-smoking campaign. They contacted journalists and gave them examples of the messages that they would be circulating.

The journalists were fascinated by the new campaign. They were eager to publicize it. However, they needed a catchy phrase to describe it: they referred to it as *fat shaming*.

Enthusiasts

Some persons had criticized the original obesity campaign because of its rhetoric. They noted that it had depicted body weight as a complicated problem for which obese persons had limited responsibility. They believed that the tone of this message had been much too soft. They preferred the harder messages associated with fat shaming.

Critics had an additional reason to criticize the earlier campaign. They had disliked the way that it had dealt with overweight families. They explained that it had encouraged parents to give dietary advice to their children. They questioned how this advice could be credible since it came from overweight parents.

Although the critics were eager to commence a fat-shaming campaign, they expected it to be controversial. They defended it by pointing out that this type of campaign had been used successfully to discourage smoking. They expected it to successfully discourage obesity.

Skeptics

Enthusiasts wondered how persons were reacting to the fat-shaming campaign. They were interested in businesspeople. They believed that those who were selling weight-loss products and services would be supportive.

The enthusiasts were correct about the weight-loss marketers. However, they had failed to consider how another segment of the business community would react.

Some businesspeople had been selling different sorts of products to obese individuals. For example, they sold "plus-sized" garments to them. Needless to say, they did not wish to see their clients chastened by fat-shaming messages.

Psychologists were another group that was skeptical of fat shaming. They explained that obese persons lived in a society in which fit and slender bodies were worshipped. They warned that fat shaming was exacerbating the guilt that they were feeling and leading to severe emotional problems.

Medical doctors came up with another reason to reject fat shaming. They noted that it depicted obesity as the result of voluntary actions. They countered that obesity could be the result of genes, metabolism, and factors over which persons had little, if any, control.

COMPUTER SHAMING

At the beginning of the twenty-first century, tech experts wished to do something that, at the time, seemed radical: equip all classrooms with computers that were connected to the internet.

The tech experts had confidence in their plan. Nonetheless, they recognized that it would be extremely expensive. They realized that they would need allies to implement it. They tried to recruit them through a public information campaign.

The experts needed an attention-getting message to highlight during their campaign. They stated that parents who sent their children to schools with good tech could expect to see three important benefits. Their children would be more motivated, perform better academically, and become eligible for high-paying jobs.

Enthusiasts

The tech experts waited to see whether schools with scant or obsolete technology would change as a result of their public information campaign. They were disappointed when many of them did not change.

The tech experts decided to alter their message. Instead of praising parents who sent their children to schools with good tech, they were going to shame those who sent their children to schools with poor tech.

The experts explained to the parents that schools could be sorted along a *digital divide*—those with computers and those without them. They contended that those parents who patronized schools on the "wrong side" of this divide were harming their children. They predicted that their children would feel the effects of that damage when they later entered the workplace.

The experts made their messages especially ominous for the parents of minority students. They stated that their children were attending schools that had been the victims of tech discrimination. They warned that their children would never catch up to peers who attended better-equipped schools.

The tech experts hoped that parents would be moved by the computer-shaming campaign. They hoped that they then would demand tech upgrades.

The parents were moved. Many of them demanded modern and plentiful equipment in the schools. They also demanded high-speed internet service, technical training for teachers, and computer coding classes for children.

The tech experts were concerned about parents. However, they were also concerned about businesspeople. They realized that the businesspeople had an enormous influence on school funding guidelines. They noted that the businesspeople had strongly endorsed their original public information campaign. They expected them to endorse their computer-shaming campaign as well.

The businesspeople did support the computer-shaming campaign. They collaborated with tech experts and parents to make sure that politicians made school tech a high priority for educational funding.

Skeptics

Parents were moved by computer shaming. An astounding 90 percent demanded not only computers in every school but also computer coding classes.

Even though most parents became computer enthusiasts, some remined skeptical. The skeptics had questions about the money that was being earmarked for computers. They wondered whether it could be spent more wisely.

The skeptics pointed out that most high schoolers, including those from poor communities, had smartphones. They questioned whether they needed additional devices at the expense of schools.

The skeptics were especially suspicious of computer coding classes. They noted that they had been characterized as ways to promote problem solving, academic achievement, and career prospects. They countered that they might be just silly fads.

POSING QUESTIONS ABOUT PUBLIC INFORMATION CAMPAIGNS

This section of the chapter contains four questions. These questions focus on the two case studies in this chapter.

The first case study concerned health experts. These experts used a public information campaign to stress the benefits of maintaining ideal weights. They hoped that it would cause persons to lose weight.

The health experts eventually concluded that their campaign was not having a significant impact on obesity. They therefore switched tactics: they tried to shame obese persons into losing weight.

While the first case study in this chapter concerned health experts, the second one focused on tech experts. These experts used a public information campaign to stress the benefits of sending children to well-equipped schools. They hoped that it would cause parents to demand upgraded equipment.

The tech experts were disappointed in their campaign. They concluded that it was not having a significant impact on the many poorly equipped schools. They therefore shifted tactics: they tried to shame parents who were sending their children to poorly equipped schools.

The questions at the end of this chapter, as well as those at the ends of subsequent chapters, will assist you if are going through this book on your own. They will give you opportunities to simulate participation in college classrooms where professors are using the case method.

Professors who use the case method direct students to examine two related incidents. They are not surprised if they don't detect the relationships between them. They then use questions to guide their analyses.

Although the following questions will help you if you are going through this book on your own, they also will help you if you are participating in actual courses.

Question 1: Why Did Health Experts Organize a Public Information Campaign about Ideal Body Weights?

Health experts organized a public information campaign about the benefits of ideal body weights. They believed that it would have an impact on the public's attitudes and behaviors.

How did different groups respond to these experts? Focus on two groups: obese persons and businesspeople.

Did obese persons have low confidence, moderate confidence, or high confidence in the way that the experts were behaving? How did businesspeople feel? Explain the bases for your answers.

When answering these questions, as well as those that follow, you can rely on the information in this chapter. You also might rely on some of the sources that are identified in the references at the back of the book. If you are reading this chapter with colleagues, you are encouraged to converse with them about the best way to answer the questions.

Question 2: Why Did Health Experts Switch to Fat Shaming?

Health experts were disappointed with the impact of their public information campaign. They hoped that fat shaming would be more effective.

How did different groups respond to these experts? Focus on two groups: obese persons and businesspeople.

Did obese persons have low confidence, moderate confidence, or high confidence in the way that the experts were behaving? How did businesspeople feel? Explain the bases for your answers.

Question 3: Why Did Tech Experts Organize a Public Information Campaign about Well-Equipped Schools?

Tech experts organized a public information campaign about the benefits of well-equipped schools. They believed that it would have an impact on the public's attitudes and behaviors.

How did different groups respond to these experts? Focus on two groups: parents and businesspeople.

Did the parents have low confidence, moderate confidence, or high confidence in the way that the experts were behaving? How did businesspeople feel? Explain the bases for your answers.

Question 4: Why Did Tech Experts Switch to Computer Shaming?

Tech experts were disappointed with the impact of their public information campaign. They hoped that computer shaming would be more effective.

How did different groups respond to these experts? Focus on two groups: parents and businesspeople.

Did the parents have low confidence, moderate confidence, or high confidence in the way that the experts were behaving? How did businesspeople feel? Explain the bases for your answers.

SUMMARY

Health experts organized a public information campaign about the benefits of ideal body weights. Tech experts organized one about the benefits of well-equipped schools. Disappointed by the results, both groups shifted to shame-inducing campaigns.

TWO

Do Angelinos Have the Right Idea about School Tech?

[The LA superintendent is spending] more than $1 billion to buy an iPad for every student.
— Journalist Tod Newcombe, 2015

[The school iPads are] really not making a difference [in student learning].
— Los Angeles Unified School District Committee Member Stuart Magruder, 2014

[There are questions the LA superintendent] should have asked long before [he bought] a single iPad.
— Journalist Sie Lapowsky, 2015

The Los Angeles schools chief . . . [has been forced to resign because of] mounting criticism.
— Journalist Motoko Rich, 2014

The administrators at Harvard used a formula to admit students. They assumed that it would promote racial diversity. The superintendent in Los Angeles bought an iPad for every student. He assumed that the purchases would promote tech learning. In both cases, they were shocked by the actual consequences.

COMPLEX CONSEQUENCES OF UNIVERSITY ADMISSIONS

Many persons applied to Harvard each year. They believed that graduating from this storied university would guarantee them successful careers.

The administrators at Harvard University had more applicants than they could admit. They carefully examined their scholastic records to determine which ones could attend.

Many of the persons who applied had truly remarkable academic credentials. When they were rejected, they were surprised that they had not made the cut. They wondered whether they had been treated fairly.

Harvard was not the first school at which applicants questioned the admission practices. During the 1970s, administrators at the University of California had to deal with an applicant who sued them because of their admission practices. They were shocked when this applicant pursued his case all the way to the US Supreme Court.

The Supreme Court's justices sided with the applicant. They disapproved of the California administrators' reason for rejecting him. They concluded that they had used de facto racial quotas. They required them to make changes to their admission practices.

Although the justices explicitly forbade the California administrators from employing racial quotas, they did not prohibit them from promoting racial diversity. They told them that they still could use race as an admission factor as long as they did not make it the determining factor.

The administrators at Harvard realized that they also had to follow the justices' guidelines. Although they still intended to collect information about applicants' races, they were going to supplement it with information about their precollegiate grades, standardized test scores, professional aspirations, social habits, community activities, and personalities.

The administrators created a formula that collapsed all of the data into a score. They used this score to determine which applicants were admitted.

Enthusiasts

The administrators acknowledged that they were using an admissions formula. Nonetheless, they refused to disclose it.

The administrators wondered how persons were reacting to their secret admission formula. They kept their eyes on the major donors to their university. They hoped they would be pleased.

The donors were pleased. They noted that the members of their families were being admitted at a rate five times greater than the persons from nondonor families. They heartily endorsed the secret formula.

The administrators also kept their eyes on government officials. They realized that they were examining whether their formula was in line with federal judicial guidelines. They were relieved when the officials concluded that their formula was in compliance.

Skeptics

The Harvard administrators were happy with their secret admissions formula. They noted that it had pleased donors, placated government watchdogs, and promoted a diversified student body.

Not everyone was happy with the formula. Some unsuccessful applicants had reservations about it. They demanded details.

The administrators calmly replied that they would not divulge details to disgruntled applicants. They remained calm even after some applicants threatened to sue.

The administrators realized that they might have to appear in court. They did not anticipate that they would have to present their formula. However, they did anticipate that they would have to present data about the manner in which that formula was affecting applicants.

The administrators turned to the office of institutional research on their campus. They asked its staff to review the impact that their formula was having on applicants.

The researchers were eager to assist. They began by computing the rejection rate for all applicants, which was greater than 90 percent. They believed that this high figure was reassuring because it explained why Harvard had so many disgruntled applicants.

As the researchers continued to analyze the impact of the admissions formula, they eventually detected an unsettling pattern. The formula was penalizing Asian Americans.

The researchers recognized that the pattern they had documented in their reports would be controversial. They therefore gave the report exclusively to Harvard's administrators. They had no reason to believe that it would be seen by anyone else.

The report was not as secure as the researchers had believed. It fell into the hands of rejected Asian American applicants, who adduced it as evidence of racial discrimination.

COMPLEX CONSEQUENCES OF IPAD-BASED INSTRUCTION

Ambitious educators were on the lookout for better jobs. They agreed that the Los Angeles Unified School District (LAUSD) presented some of the best opportunities. They found the superintendent's job especially appealing.

Although this superintendent's position involved amazing opportunities, it also encompassed some unnerving perils. It had been occupied by three individuals from 2000 to 2011. None of the occupants had lasted more than six years.

John Deasy knew that the LAUSD's top position could be perilous. Nonetheless, he still wanted it. He lobbied aggressively for it. He was ecstatic after he secured it.

Deasy became superintendent in 2011. He immediately stated that he would be making changes. He wanted these changes to transform the district. He also wanted them to extend his tenure as superintendent. He believed that tech changes had the best chance of achieving these goals.

Deasy announced that he would be purchasing sophisticated administrative software. He explained that this software would track students quickly, cheaply, and accurately.

Deasy was asked about the price of the software. Although he admitted that it would be high, he contended that it would pay for itself with the money that it saved on clerical salaries.

Journalists wanted more details. They noted that Deasy had estimated the software's price at less than 100 million dollars. After they had made their own investigation, they discovered that it would be significantly higher — possibly double Deasy's estimate.

The journalists concluded that the administrative software was not especially cost effective. However, they found another fault with it: it was not especially efficient. They located administrators, teachers, and high school students who had piloted it and judged that it was slow and error prone.

Deasy wondered how parents were reacting to the information from critical journalists. Although he was relieved when they seemed to ignore the criticism, he was disappointed when they also ignored his new software.

Deasy was ready to make another tech change. However, he wished to make sure that this one attracted more public interest than his last one. He decided to focus on student learning rather than administrator efficiency.

Deasy contended that children were at an academic disadvantage when they did not have computers or tablets. He had a solution for this problem: he was going to give them personal iPads.

Deasy was asked about the price for the iPads. He acknowledged that it would be high. However, he pledged to lower it by negotiating a special deal with the Apple Corporation.

Deasy worried that many persons would think that the cost of the iPads, even after discounts, was too high. He urged them to focus on the educational benefits of the devices rather than the cost. He stated that these benefits were so evident that he would "make no apologies" for the money that he was spending.

Enthusiasts

Deasy was interested in the community's reactions to the iPad purchase. He was especially interested in the reactions of businesspeople, journalists, and parents.

The businesspeople had been enthusiastic about the administrative software purchases. They were enthusiastic about the iPad purchases as well. They noted that they reflected the innovations that they were making in their own operations. They concluded that were not only appropriate but long overdue.

Journalists had not been impressed by the administrative software. However, they were supportive of the iPads. Those who had been writing about the digital divide in schools were particularly supportive. They portrayed the massive iPad purchase as a bold attempt to bridge this divide.

Journalists gave extensive coverage to the iPads. They aimed their reporting at parents. They encouraged them to be supportive.

Parents were generally supportive. However, they wanted to know the precise amount for the purchase.

Skeptics

Journalists were eager to give the parents more information. They began by investigating the amount that the superintendent had budgeted for iPads.

The journalists noted that Deasy had estimated that the district needed several hundred million dollars to cover the cost of the equipment. However, they realized that he had not included the amount needed to upgrade internet service, expand instructor training, and add auxiliary personnel. They estimated that the total amount for the purchase would be more than a billion dollars. They changed their minds about the appropriateness of the purchase.

The parents were astounded at the difference between the initial estimate and the actual cost. Some of them believed that Deasy had deliberately deceived them in order to help business cronies. They asked the Securities and Exchange Commission to investigate him. In the meantime, they implored the school board to fire him.

RESPONDING TO QUESTIONS ABOUT COMPLEX CONSEQUENCES

Administrators at Harvard relied on a formula to guide them when they were admitting students. They assumed that it was promoting racial diversity.

A superintendent bought an iPad for every student in Los Angeles. He assumed that these purchases were promoting tech learning.

In both cases, the individuals believed that their plans would be hugely popular. They were shocked when they became controversial.

The events at Harvard and in Los Angeles were not interrelated. Nonetheless, they had some similarities. After you answer the following questions, see if you discern those similarities.

Question 1: Why Did Harvard Administrators Use a Formula to Guide Admissions?

University administrators used a formula to decide which applicants they would accept at Harvard. They believed that this formula would expand racial diversity.

How did different groups respond to these university administrators? Focus on two groups: donors and applicants.

Did the donors have low confidence, moderate confidence, or high confidence in the way that these university administrators were behaving? How did the applicants feel? Explain the bases for your answers.

When answering these questions, as well as those that follow, you can rely on the information in this chapter. You also might rely on some of the sources that are identified in the references at the back of the book. If you are reading this chapter with colleagues, you are encouraged to converse with them about the best way to answer the questions.

Question 2: Why Were Harvard Administrators Faulted for their Admissions Formula?

The university administrators had anticipated how their admissions formula would affect some racial minority groups. However, they were criticized for failing to anticipate how it would specifically affect Asian American applicants.

How did different groups respond to these university administrators? Focus on two groups: donors and applicants.

Did the donors have low confidence, moderate confidence, or high confidence in the way that these university administrators were behaving? How did the applicants feel? Explain the bases for your answers.

Question 3: Why Did an LA Superintendent Purchase an iPad for Every Student?

A superintendent resolved to purchase an iPad for every student in Los Angeles. He believed that the purchases would expand tech learning.

How did different groups respond to this superintendent? Focus on two groups: parents and businesspeople.

Did the parents have low confidence, moderate confidence, or high confidence in the way that this superintendent was behaving? How did the businesspeople feel? Explain the bases for your answers.

Question 4: Why Was the LA Superintendent Faulted for the iPad Purchases?

The superintendent calculated the amount needed to purchase an iPad for every student. However, he was criticized for failing to include the amount needed for internet service, instructor training, and auxiliary personnel.

How did different groups respond to this superintendent? Focus on two groups: parents and businesspeople.

Did the parents have low confidence, moderate confidence, or high confidence in the way that this superintendent was behaving? How did the businesspeople feel? Explain the bases for your answers.

SUMMARY

University administrators devised a plan to promote racial diversity at Harvard. A superintendent devised a plan to promote tech learning in Los Angeles. In both cases, they failed to anticipate the complex consequences of their plans.

THREE

Do Detroiters Have the Right Idea about School Tech?

[Our schools desperately need] classrooms wired for the internet.
—Detroit Federation of Teachers, 2007

I had six laptops for 42 fifth-grade students.
—Detroit Teacher Kelsey Pavelka, 2018

We've had a total and complete collapse of education in this city.
—Detroit Lawyer Scott Romney, 2017

[This school] district is committed to providing all students . . . with computer science [training].
—Detroit Superintendent Nikolai Vitti, 2018

Elected officials were under pressure to fix local roads. They searched for a solution that was cheap, effective, and appealing to constituents. They believed that road diets had these characteristics.

The superintendent in Detroit was under pressure to fix school problems. He searched for a solution that was cheap, effective, and appealing to constituents. He believed that universal computer science training had these characteristics.

ROAD DIETS AS INEXPENSIVE CURE-ALLS

Residents in every community paid attention to their roads. They could not help but be mindful of them when they were driving, bicycling, or walking on them. They were upset when the roads had problems.

Residents were upset because road problems made it difficult for them to get around quickly and safely. They expected them to be fixed. They complained to elected officials when they were not.

The elected officials listened respectfully to their constituents. They assured them that their engineers would devise a solution.

The engineers did have a solution. They wished to demolish problematic roads and replace them with better-designed ones. They stated that this plan would be highly effective.

Residents liked the engineers' plan. However, they wanted to know the amount it would cost.

The elected officials replied that demolishing and replacing roads would be costly. They told them that they would try to convince taxpayers to cover the expenses.

The elected officials had little luck with the taxpayers. They realized that they would need a cheaper solution for road problems. They again consulted the engineers.

The engineers came up with an alternative plan. They could transform multilane roads into two-lane roads. They were sure that this would alter traffic flow, speed up travel times, reduce road maintenance expenses, and improve safety.

The elected officials liked the cheaper plan. They searched for an easy-to-understand phrase with which to describe it. They experimented with *roadway reconfiguration, road rechannelization,* and *traffic calming*. However, they finally settled on *road diets*.

Enthusiasts

The elected officials were excited about road diets. They hoped that their constituents would share their excitement. They waited to see their reaction.

Most constituents had concluded that demolition and reconstruction was the best solution for road problems. Nonetheless, they were not willing to cover the cost. They therefore switched their support to road diets.

Bicyclists and walkers were especially supportive of the road diets. They liked the concept of reducing the space available to motorists and reassigning it to them. They anticipated that they would be safer as a result.

Skeptics

Commuters who used buses had doubts about the road diets. They worried that their buses would have greater difficulty leaving and entering lanes. They predicted that they would run slower as a result.

Some motorists were skeptical of the road diets. They believed that they would be inefficient. They predicted that they would be especially inefficient when residents were fleeing from wildfires, storms, or other natural disasters.

Businesspeople from the construction industry were disappointed with road diets. They had an extremely practical reason: they would be making a smaller profit from them than they would have made from demolition and reconstruction.

UNIVERSAL COMPUTER SCIENCE TRAINING AS AN INEXPENSIVE CURE-ALL

The schools in Detroit had over 270,000 students during the early 1970s. They had only one-third as many twenty-five years later.

The teachers were anxious about the students who had left Detroit's schools. They were forced to close buildings, lay off staff, and reduce services. They were not sure that they could meet the needs of the students who remained. They complained to their school leaders.

The school leaders listened as teachers described their problems. However, they hardly needed their testimonials to be convinced. They pointed out that the city's many vacant homes, shuttered factories, and closed retail businesses indicated the larger scope of those problems.

The teachers agreed that the entire city had problems. Nonetheless, they still wanted the school leaders to find solutions to the problems in their classrooms. They were not the only ones.

Michigan's governor and legislators demanded that Detroit's school leaders take action. They eventually became so exasperated with them that they stripped them of their authority and reassigned it to emergency managers.

Detroit's local school leaders lost their authority in 2009. They remained out of power for seven years. They were excited when they eventually regained it. Nonetheless, they recognized that they had to show demonstrable educational progress to retain it.

The leaders agreed on the first step that they should take: they had to appoint a superintendent. They selected an experienced administrator — Nikolai Vitti.

Superintendent Vitti knew that he and the persons who had hired him were in precarious positions. He concluded that they would need a transformational educational plan to bolster their security.

The superintendent was not intimidated by the challenge before him. He had just left Jacksonville, Florida, a city with its own daunting challenges. He had proposed technology as the solution for the challenges.

Vitti had directed the Jacksonville teachers to switch from paper textbooks to digital materials. He assured them that they then would be preparing students for high-tech jobs and saving the district money.

The Jacksonville teachers had been nervous about Vitti's plan. They did not have enough computers to implement it properly. When they were unable to change the superintendent's mind, they resisted him. After recruiting parents as their allies, they forced the superintendent to abandon his plan.

Vitti had been frustrated after he was unable to implement his tech-centered plan in Jacksonville. Nonetheless, he wondered whether he should try the same plan in Detroit.

The state-appointed managers had supervised Detroit's teachers before Vitti arrived. They had told them to abandon printed textbooks and replace them with eTextbooks. Similar to the events in Jacksonville, they had to abandon this plan because the teachers did not have enough computers.

Vitti concluded that his Jacksonville plan was too similar to the one that had already been tried in Detroit. Nonetheless, he still believed that some type of tech plan was the key to solving the city's school problems.

Vitti needed another plan. He quickly settled on one that had never been tried in Detroit. He stated that he would implement universal tech training. He explained that he would be providing every student with the opportunity to enroll in computer science courses.

Enthusiasts

Vitti waited to see how persons would respond to universal computer science training. He was particularly concerned about businesspeople and parents.

The businesspeople were supportive. They believed the training would create a pool of highly qualified workers. They hoped that it would enable them to scale back some of the costly training programs that they had been funding for employees.

Parents also were supportive. They anticipated that their children would graduate from high school with computer skills and then qualify for rewarding jobs.

Skeptics

Superintendent Vitti was pleased with the reactions of businesspeople and parents to his plan. However, he also was concerned about teachers.

The teachers listened carefully to their superintendent's plan. However, they had heard similar ambitious plans from former superintendents and the state-appointed managers. Because they had been disappointed by these groups, they were skeptical of Vitti's plan.

The teachers urged Vitti to take several steps before implementing universal computer science training. They believed that two of these steps were obvious: he should get more computers for the schools and upgrade internet service.

The teachers doubted that Vitti had the funds to buy computers or to improve internet service. They anticipated that he would have to persuade the city's cash-strapped residents to supply them. After noting that former superintendents and the state-appointed managers had failed to persuade them, they predicted that he also would fail.

The teachers suggested that Vitti develop some nontech goals. For example, they told him to make sure that their classrooms had freshly painted walls, their hallways had functioning drinking fountains, and they had equitable salaries.

RESPONDING TO QUESTIONS ABOUT RHETORICAL EUPHEMISMS

Elected officials were under pressure to fix roads. They looked for a solution that would be cheap, effective, and appealing to their constituents. They believed that *road diets* had these characteristics.

A superintendent in Detroit was under pressure to fix school problems. He looked for a solution that would be cheap, effective, and appealing to his constituents. He believed that *universal computer science training* had these characteristics.

Attempts to fix road problems and school problems were unrelated. Nonetheless, they had some similarities. After you answer the following questions, see if you discern those similarities.

Question 1: Why Did Elected Officials Support Road Construction Projects?

Elected officials fretted over problematic roads in their community. They historically had recommended costly construction projects because they believed that they were the most effective antidotes.

How did different groups respond to these elected officials? Focus on two groups: community residents and businesspeople.

Did the residents have low confidence, moderate confidence, or high confidence in the way that the officials were behaving? How did the businesspeople feel? Explain the bases for your answers.

When answering these questions, as well as those that follow, you can rely on the information in this chapter. You also might rely on some of the sources that are identified in the references at the back of the book. If you are reading this chapter with colleagues, you are encouraged to converse with them about the best way to answer the questions.

Question 2: Why Did Elected Officials Switch Their Support to Road Diets?

Elected officials could not convince their constituents to fund costly construction projects. They therefore switched their support to road diets as a cheaper-to-implement alternative.

How did different groups respond to these elected officials? Focus on two groups: community residents and businesspeople.

Did the residents have low confidence, moderate confidence, or high confidence in the way that the officials were behaving? How did the businesspeople feel? Explain the bases for your answers.

Question 3: Why Did Superintendents in Detroit Support Tech Upgrades?

Superintendents in Detroit fretted over problematic schools in their community. They historically had recommended costly tech upgrades because they believed that they were the most effective antidotes.

How did different groups respond to these superintendents? Focus on two groups: teachers and businesspeople.

Did the teachers have low confidence, moderate confidence, or high confidence in the way that the superintendents were behaving? How did the businesspeople feel? Explain the bases for your answers.

Question 4: Why Did a Superintendent in Detroit Switch His Support to Universal Computer Science Training?

Detroit's superintendents could not convince their constituents to fund costly tech upgrades. One of them therefore switched his support to universal computer science training as a cheaper-to-implement alternative.

How did different groups respond to this superintendent? Focus on two groups: teachers and businesspeople.

Did the teachers have low confidence, moderate confidence, or high confidence in the way that this superintendent was behaving? How did the businesspeople feel? Explain the bases for your answers.

SUMMARY

Elected officials fretted over problematic roads in their community. They searched for a solution that was cheap, effective, and appealing to their constituents. They believed that road diets had all of these characteristics.

A superintendent fretted over problematic schools in Detroit. He searched for a solution that was cheap, effective, and appealing to his constituents. He believed that universal computer science training had all of these characteristics.

FOUR
Do Miamians Have the Right Idea about School Tech?

[A Miami student hacked into his] school website to change his grades.
—Journalist Kyle Munzenrieder, 2014

[Another] Miami student is facing felony charges after allegedly hacking into his school website.
—Journalist Gillian Mohney, 2014

[The student hacker I am representing in court is] a very smart kid . . . [and] a hard worker.
—Miami Attorney Steven Saad, 2017

[The high school computer science] curriculum . . . is being revamped to ensure that [student hacking does] not occur in the future.
—Miami Schools Media Director Jackie Calzadilla, 2018

A Miami superintendent repeatedly interviewed for positions in other communities. Although he pledged that he would cease, he could not convince skeptics.

Students in Miami's computer science classes repeatedly hacked into school websites. Although they pledged that they would cease, they could not convince skeptics.

PREDICTING THE BEHAVIOR OF A SCHOOL LEADER

Miami-Dade is one of the largest school districts in the country. It has multiple teachers, numerous students, and a multi-billion-dollar budget. It attracts top-notch applicants for administrative positions.

Alberto Carvalho was eager to secure the Miami-Dade superintendent's position. He applied for it in 2008. He beamed when he was successful.

Carvalho received enormous attention because of the position that he occupied. However, he received just as much attention because of the personal traits he exhibited. He was bright, articulate, and collegial.

Enthusiasts

Carvalho developed a reputation that extended across the country. He spoke at influential conferences and presented his views over major media outlets. He surprised few persons when he was selected as the national Superintendent of the Year.

Bill de Blasio was the mayor of New York City. He was aware of Carvalho's reputation. When his city's Chancellor of Education job became available in 2018, he resolved to offer it to Carvalho.

Skeptics

The mayor anticipated that he would need help to recruit the charismatic superintendent. He asked local journalists to assist him. They were eager to lend a hand. They believed that Carvalho had the "star power" to bring unprecedented excitement to their city's massive educational bureaucracy.

The journalists at the *New York Times* may have been the most enthusiastic. They released a flood of flattering reports. They made it clear that Carvalho exceeded all of their expectations for a Chancellor of Education.

The mayor's aides realized that their boss was entranced by Carvalho. Nonetheless, they urged him to be cautious. They reminded him of the way Carvalho had behaved when he was interviewing for the superintendent's job in the Tampa area.

Carvalho had left the impression that he would accept the Tampa job. However, he had requested additional time before announcing his decision. He then used that time to secure the Miami superintendent's job.

Mayor de Blasio dismissed the warnings about Carvalho. He was excited when Carvalho agreed to come to New York City for an interview. He believed he could recruit him.

At the end of Carvalho's interview, de Blasio offered him the position. He then met with reporters and told them that Carvalho had accepted the offer and soon would be making an announcement.

The mayor became uneasy when Carvalho delayed the announcement. He became even more uneasy when Carvalho indicated that he was ready to make the announcement but that he wished to make it during a live broadcast.

During that broadcast, Carvalho addressed his remarks to Miamians. He told them that he had the opportunity to serve as Educational Chancellor of New York City. He explained that this was a once-in-a-lifetime opportunity. He assured them that he had carefully deliberated about it. However, he told them that he was turning it down because he was too committed to them, their children, and his current job.

Carvalho expected that Miamians would be watching his broadcast. He felt confident about their reactions: they would prize him more than ever.

Carvalho knew that Mayor de Blasio also would be watching his broadcast. He was equally sure about his reaction: he would be furious.

PREDICTING THE BEHAVIOR OF COMPUTER SCIENCE STUDENTS

Alberto Carvalho had become Miami's superintendent in 2008. He had wished to immediately make a positive impression on his constituents. He had looked at school leaders in other communities for ideas about the strategies that they had used.

Carvalho was struck by the frequency with which school leaders had relied on technology to create positive impressions. He noted that they had begun by aggressively expanding the number of computers in their districts. He resolved to copy them.

Although Carvalho was ready to buy computers, he faced a problem. He was out of money. He had just slashed his operating budget by two billion dollars.

Carvalho was still in a good mood. He had learned that Governor Rick Scott was making special funds available for school computers in the Florida schools.

Carvalho was in a good mood because of the money that Scott was providing. However, he became in a much better mood after he learned about some additional money that President Barack Obama was providing.

Obama announced in 2014 that several technology companies would be donating more than one-half-billion dollars of equipment to the schools. He was supplementing their donation with two billion dollars of federal funds for high-speed internet services and four billion dollars for computer science classes.

Enthusiasts

Carvalho made plans to replace outdated school computers, acquire high-speed internet, and expand computer science classes. He announced that he would be relying on state and federal funds. He then waited to see how his constituents responded. He focused on the local elected officials and businesspeople.

The local elected officials applauded the announcement. They depicted Carvalho as a visionary leader who was using technology to transform their schools. They especially admired him for procuring state and federal resources to pay for this transformation.

The local businesspeople also applauded the announcement from Carvalho. They were especially excited about the computer coding classes. They needed the graduates of those classes for tech jobs at their firms.

Carvalho could not have been more pleased by the reactions of the elected officials and businesspeople. He recognized how important they were to his tenure as superintendent. However, he did not doubt that parents were just as important. He investigated their reactions to his plans.

The parents told the superintendent that they were excited about his plans. They were especially excited about the plan to offer more computer coding classes. They wanted their children to enroll in them, develop sophisticated skills, and then secure higher-waged jobs.

Skeptics

Miami residents did not doubt that students were developing sophisticated skills in their computer coding courses. However, they changed their minds about the value of those skills after they discovered how students were using them.

The students were applying their skills to problems that the instructors had not anticipated. For example, they had cracked the security codes for the administrative computers at their schools and then were changing grades.

Local journalists wanted information about the student hackers. They easily found details about those who had been arrested and charged. However, they were able to acquire additional information about some who had never been charged.

The journalists depicted the student hackers as criminals who were threatening the schools and the community. They demanded that the superintendent deal with them. They were joined by parents. They peppered the superintendent with questions about the steps that he was going to take.

The superintendent stated that he had purchased special antihacking software. He was certain that it would protect the schools' computers.

The superintendent added that he had taken still another step. He had directed all computer science teachers to provide students with additional instruction about ethical behavior.

POSING QUESTIONS ABOUT RECURRING PATTERNS

The superintendent of Miami impressed constituents with the way that he handled his job. Nonetheless, he distressed them when he applied for jobs in other communities. Although he promised to stay in Miami, he continued to go for job interviews.

Students in Miami impressed city residents with the way that they handled their computer science classes. Nonetheless, they distressed them when they hacked into their schools' computers. Although they promised to act ethically, they still engaged in hacking.

The actions of the Miami superintendent while interviewing for jobs and those of his students while hacking into computers were not interrelated. Nonetheless, they had some similarities. After you answer the following questions, see if you discern those similarities.

Question 1: How Did Miami's Superintendent Deal with Challenges in Local Schools?

Superintendent Carvalho faced challenges in Miami's schools. He demonstrated impressive administrative skills while dealing with them.

How did different groups respond to the superintendent? Focus on two groups: journalists and parents.

Did the journalists have low confidence, moderate confidence, or high confidence in the way that the superintendent was behaving? How did the parents feel? Explain the bases for your answers.

When answering these questions, as well as those that follow, you can rely on the information in this chapter. You also might rely on some of the sources that are identified in the references at the back of the book. If you are reading this chapter with colleagues, you are encouraged to converse with them about the best way to answer the questions.

Question 2: How Did Miami's Superintendent Deal with Challenges in the Schools of Other Districts?

Superintendent Carvalho had opportunities to address challenges in other school districts. Although he even interviewed for jobs in those districts, he turned down the job offers and promised to stay in Miami.

How did different groups respond to the superintendent? Focus on two groups: journalists and parents.

Did the journalists have low confidence, moderate confidence, or high confidence in the way that the superintendent was behaving? How did the parents feel? Explain the bases for your answers.

Question 3: How Did Miami's Students Deal with Challenges in Computer Science Classes?

Miami's students faced challenges in their computer science classes. They demonstrated impressive skills while dealing with them.

How did different groups respond to the students? Focus on two groups: journalists and parents.

Did the journalists have low confidence, moderate confidence, or high confidence in the way that the students were behaving? How did the parents feel? Explain the bases for your answers.

Question 4: How Did Miami's Students Deal with Challenges in the Administrative Computers at their Schools?

Miami's students had opportunities to hack into the administrative computers at their schools. Although they took advantage of those opportunities, they expressed remorse and promised to behave ethically.

How did different groups respond to the students? Focus on two groups: journalists and parents.

Did the journalists have low confidence, moderate confidence, or high confidence in the way that the students were behaving? How did the parents feel? Explain the bases for your answers.

SUMMARY

A superintendent in Miami demonstrated impressive administrative skills. He had chances to apply those skills in other communities. Even though he interviewed for jobs in those communities, he turned them down and pledged to focus his attention on Miami.

Students in Miami's computer science classes demonstrated impressive skills. They had chances to use those skills to hack the administrative computers at their schools. Even though they did hack into those computers, they expressed remorse and promised to focus their attention on their classes.

FIVE

Do Philadelphians Have the Right Idea about School Tech?

[A Philadelphia-area superintendent] provided 2,300 high-school students with Mac laptops.
—Journalist Daniel Nasaw, 2010

[The Mac laptops had spy cameras that] captured more than 50,000 images of students.
—Journalist Ewen MacAskill, 2010

I don't feel this school has the right to put cameras inside the kids' home, inside their bedrooms, and spy on them.
—Parent Holly Robbins, 2010

[The spy cameras were to be] activated only to help locate a lost or stolen laptop.
—Philadelphia-Area Superintendent Christopher McGinley, 2010

Entrepreneurs offered university diplomas that did not require traditional coursework. They insisted that they were comparable to the diplomas from reputable universities.

A Philadelphia-area superintendent offered free laptops. He insisted that they were comparable to the laptops from reputable suppliers.

QUESTIONABLE DIPLOMAS

International students were eager to attend universities in the United States. They were convinced that graduation from them would lead to prestigious careers and high-salaried jobs.

Some of the international students did not have the money to pay for the tuition and fees at American universities. Although they could earn money by letting their college coursework lapse and taking jobs, they have to be careful not to jeopardize their student visas.

Pakistani entrepreneurs were aware of the challenges that the international students faced. They were ready to help them. They assured students that their company, Axact, could help them enroll in a highly regarded university.

The entrepreneurs created an enticing website that featured the universities they represented. They filled it with photos of impressive buildings, spacious lecture halls, well-equipped labs, verdurous grounds, energetic students, and engaged faculty. They also included testimonials from students who had earned diplomas and secured high-paying jobs.

The entrepreneurs provided another incentive to prospective students. They told them that they would not have to complete traditional academic courses. They explained that they could receive academic credit for their day-to-day experiences at their jobs. They emphasized that they then would be able to maintain full-time jobs while they earned their degrees. They also emphasized that their degrees, even though they were earned in nontraditional manners, would be comparable to the degrees from the most respected universities.

Enthusiasts

The entrepreneurs hoped that prospective students would examine the Axact website. They were eager to see how they then would respond.

International students in the United States did examine the website. They realized that they were being offered the opportunity to hold full-time jobs, avoid onerous coursework, earn college diplomas, and retain their foreign student visas. They were enticed.

Many students enrolled at Axact. In fact, so many enrolled that they soon were paying millions of dollars to the firm.

Skeptics

Journalists became interested in Axact. They wondered how it was able to offer diplomas to students who had not completed any formal academic coursework. They decided to investigate.

The journalists wished to visit Axact's executives at their head office, which had an address in Pakistan. However, they could not locate the building. They also could not locate any of the campuses that were identified on the Axact website.

The journalists concluded that the information on the website had been fabricated. They warned the entrepreneurs that they were about to publish an exposé.

The entrepreneurs were livid. They explained that they were giving college students an innovative way to earn academic degrees while simultaneously retaining jobs. They threatened to sue any journalist who misrepresented their efforts.

The journalists were not intimidated. They were eager to share their investigation with a wide audience.

QUESTIONABLE COMPUTERS

Christopher McGinley had several high-profile educational experiences in Philadelphia. He highlighted them when he applied to become superintendent of Lower Merion Township, a suburb of Philadelphia.

McGinley was able to secure the superintendent's position. He was eager to make a positive impression on his new constituents. He therefore set a lofty goal. He would use technology to transform their schools into a "21st-century learning environment."

Enthusiasts

McGinley had modeled his goal after one that Philadelphians had already adopted. He had been impressed with the enthusiasm that the Philadelphians had shown. He expected his own constituents to respond similarly. However, he had not fully considered how distinct the residents of these two communities were.

Many Philadelphians lived at the federal poverty line or even below it. They sent their children to schools that did not have computers or teachers who were trained to use them. In contrast, the residents of Lower Merion Township were among the wealthiest persons in America. They sent their children to schools that had abundant computers and teachers with advanced tech skills.

McGinley was hard-pressed to specify precisely how he would improve the tech in his school district. He needed a practical strategy. He finally identified one: he would give every student a laptop.

Skeptics

McGinley was not worried about paying for laptops. He had plenty of money. He resolved to buy enough computers for all high school students.

McGinley assumed that the high schoolers would be impressed when they received free personal laptops. He was shocked when they were not. He asked his staff for an explanation.

The staff explained that the students already had personal laptops. Although they might have appreciated an additional device, they hardly needed it. Moreover, their parents would likely have the same attitude.

The superintendent had not anticipated the way that students and their parents would react to free laptops. Although he was disappointed, he did not consider the problem to be a major one. However, he soon learned that this problem was being aggravated by another one.

The superintendent's own staff had created the second problem. They had contacted parents and complained about the behaviors that their children were exhibiting at home.

The parents were confused. They asked how the staff had collected information about their children while they were in their homes. They were shocked when they responded that they had gathered it with spy cameras on school-furnished laptops.

The parents contacted the superintendent. They asked if he had known about the spy cameras.

McGinley answered cautiously. He admitted that he had known about these cameras. However, he had given orders to activate them only when laptops were lost or stolen. He hoped that the parents would be satisfied with this assurance.

The parents were not satisfied. They were convinced that the superintendent was being disingenuous. They asked local journalists to express their outrage. The journalists were eager to assist.

DEALING WITH QUESTIONABLE ASSURANCES

Pakistani entrepreneurs offered coursework-free university diplomas to students. Although they insisted that the diplomas were comparable to those from reputable universities, they had difficulty convincing skeptics.

A Philadelphia-area superintendent offered free laptops to students. Although he insisted that they were comparable to those from reputable dealers, he had difficulty convincing skeptics.

The incidents with the Pakistani entrepreneurs and a Philadelphia-area superintendent were not interrelated. Nonetheless, they had some similarities. After you answer the following questions, see if you discern those similarities.

Question 1: Why Did Pakistani Entrepreneurs Offer Coursework-Free Diplomas?

Pakistani entrepreneurs offered university diplomas that did not require traditional coursework. They maintained that these diplomas, which were comparable to those from reputable universities, were components of an innovative model of higher education.

How did different groups respond to the entrepreneurs? Focus on two groups: students and journalists.

Did the students have low confidence, moderate confidence, or high confidence in the way that the entrepreneurs were behaving? How did the journalists feel? Explain the bases for your answers.

When answering these questions, as well as those that follow, you can rely on the information in this chapter. You also might rely on some of the sources that are identified in the references at the back of the book. If you are reading this chapter with colleagues, you are encouraged to converse with them about the best way to answer the questions.

Question 2: Why Did Pakistani Entrepreneurs Stop Offering Coursework-Free Diplomas?

The entrepreneurs had insisted that the coursework-free diplomas came from reputable universities. However, they stopped offering them after those universities were discovered to be fictitious.

How did different groups respond to the entrepreneurs? Focus on two groups: students and journalists.

Did the students have low confidence, moderate confidence, or high confidence in the way that the entrepreneurs were behaving? How did the journalists feel? Explain the bases for your answers.

Question 3: Why Did a Philadelphia-Area Superintendent Offer Free Laptops?

A Philadelphia-area superintendent offered free laptops to students. He maintained that the laptops, which were comparable to those from reputable retailers, were components of an innovative model of high-tech education.

How did different groups respond to the superintendent? Focus on two groups: parents and journalists.

Did the parents have low confidence, moderate confidence, or high confidence in the way that this superintendent was behaving? How did the journalists feel? Explain the bases for your answers.

Question 4: Why Did the Philadelphia-Area Superintendent Stop Offering Free Laptops?

The superintendent had insisted that the free laptops came from reputable suppliers. However, he stopped offering them after they were discovered to have spy cameras on them.

How did different groups respond to the superintendent? Focus on two groups: parents and journalists.

Did the parents have low confidence, moderate confidence, or high confidence in the way that this superintendent was behaving? How did the journalists feel? Explain the bases for your answers.

SUMMARY

Pakistani entrepreneurs offered coursework-free university diplomas to students. They claimed that they were comparable to the diplomas from reputable universities. A Philadelphia-area superintendent offered free laptops to students. He claimed that they were comparable to the laptops from reputable suppliers. In both cases, they were challenged by skeptics.

SIX
Do Tampa's Parents Have the Right Idea about School Tech?

[A greater emphasis on school safety is] the new reality that we live in.
—Tampa Bay Area Sheriff Troy Ferguson, 2018

[Schools are spending billions on] video surveillance and facial recognition software.
—Florida Citizens Alliance Blogger Domine Clemons, 2019

[I will investigate any] failure to follow . . . [the new] safety laws [that require armed personnel in every school].
—Florida Governor Rick DeSantis, 2019

There will be some unintended consequences from [the laws that require armed personnel in every school].
—Florida Representative Cynthia Stafford, 2018

Floridians wished to expand daylight savings time. They also wished to expand school safety tech. In both instances, they underestimated the resistance to these changes.

EXPANDING DAYLIGHT SAVINGS TIME

Floridians looked forward to long sunlit evenings during daylight savings time (DST). They used them to go on walks, jogs, and bicycle rides.

Floridians noticed that their evenings were extremely pleasant year-round. They wondered why they had to switch back to standard time each fall.

The Floridians investigated how other states handled time changes. They discovered that two of them, Arizona and Hawaii, did not make them at all. These states kept their clocks set to standard time throughout the year.

The Floridians wished to copy Arizona and Hawaii: they proposed to keep their clocks set to a single time. However, they preferred DST. They contacted their state legislators with this proposal.

The Floridians were disappointed when the legislators displayed little enthusiasm for their proposal. They looked for a way to put pressure on them. They contacted journalists and asked for their help.

Enthusiasts

The journalists were excited about year-round DST. They contended that it would have multiple advantages, the biggest of which would be savings on utilities.

The journalists explained that persons used less energy during DST. They reasoned that they used less during DST evenings because they had additional hours of sunlight. They figured that they used less during DST mornings because they were asleep for a good portion of them.

The journalists identified another benefit of DST. They contended that persons were healthier during this period. They explained that people used the extra daylight hours for exercise. They added that even those who went out to shop or dine benefited more than they would have if they were sedentary at home.

The journalists detected one more important benefit of year-round DST. They contended that it stimulated the economy. They explained that persons patronized stores and restaurants more often than they did when evenings were dark.

Businesspersons agreed with the journalists. Those from the tourism and recreation industries were the most ardent. They echoed the plea for year-round DST.

The proponents of year-round DST were pleased that many persons agreed with them. However, they realized that some still remained skeptical.

Skeptics

The skeptics believed that the benefits of DST had been overstated. They were sure that the savings on utilities would be less than predicted. They located experts who sided with them.

The skeptics had another concern about year-round DST. They scorned the notion that persons would be healthier as a result of it. They predicted that most persons would spend their time driving rather than walking or bicycling. To substantiate this point, they noted that the number of car accidents was greater during DST than it was during standard time.

The skeptics predicted that year-round DST would not be practicable if Florida were the only state to adopt it. They were sure that this situation would confuse residents in other states. They warned that this confusion could outweigh any benefits. They advised their state legislators to retain the current time changes.

The state legislators listened respectfully to the skeptical constituents. However, they did not follow their advice. They instead followed that from their most influential constituents—the businesspeople in the tourism and recreation industries. They promised them that they would enact a year-round DST law.

The legislators were ready to enact the law in 2019. They came up with a snappy name for it—*The Sunshine Protection Act*. They passed it and sent it to Governor Rick Scott.

Scott quickly approved *The Sunshine Protection Act*. He then forwarded it to the staff at the federal Department of Transportation, which had the final authority for the proposal.

Florida's governor and state legislators had expected the federal staff to perfunctorily approve their proposal. They were shocked when they did not. They demanded an explanation.

The staff members had a simple explanation. Although they did not doubt that the proposal would benefit persons in Florida, they believed that it would confuse persons outside of their state. They judged that this confusion would then impede interstate commerce.

The Floridians objected. They pointed out that Arizona's and Hawaii's year-round standard time had not been especially confusing. They asked why their state's year-round DST would be any more confusing.

The staff members did not give a specific reason that year-round DST was more confusing. However, they still refused to approve it.

EXPANDING SCHOOL SAFETY TECH

A Florida teen attracted international attention in 2018. He armed himself, entered his high school, and killed seventeen persons.

Floridians were shocked by this rampaging teen. They demanded that schools take steps to prevent other youths from copying him.

Educational administrators replied promptly. They stated that they would assess all current safety procedures. However, they were interrupted by their state's governor and legislators.

The governor and legislators made their own assessment of school safety procedures. They concluded that they were inadequate. Furthermore, they knew how to fix them. They wanted to place armed school resource officers (SROs) on every campus.

The administrators did not dispute the value of SROs. They were pleased that their elected officials had even provided a portion of the funds that they would need to hire them. However, they had to come up with the remainder of the funds. They did not know where to get them.

The administrators concluded that they would need cheap ways to comply with the state's directive. Some of them hired persons who had less training than the SROs. They explained that they could afford these persons, whom they referred to as guardians, because they would receive lower wages than the SROs.

Some administrators found an even cheaper way to comply with the state's directive. They armed their teachers.

Residents in Tampa Bay were aware of the three proposals for increasing school safety. They had to decide whether they would station SROs, guardians, or armed teachers on their campuses. They carefully considered the chances that these different groups had of stopping assailants. They also considered their chances of harming innocent bystanders.

The residents concluded that the SROs had the highest probability of stopping assailants. They judged that the guardians had lower probability and the armed teachers still lower. They added that the SROs also had the best chance of avoiding harm to bystanders.

Journalists were intrigued by the competing proposals for safety personnel. One of them visited a local high school to buttonhole students and get their reactions. She was particularly concerned about their reactions to arming their teachers.

One student told this journalist that she and her friends did not want their teachers to pack guns. She explained that we "barely trust teachers with grades" so "why would we trust them with a firearm?"

Businesspeople who sold school safety products sensed that Floridians could not agree about the best way to keep students safe. They therefore presented them with another proposal. They suggested that they avoid armed personnel entirely and rely instead on their products.

Enthusiasts

The businesspeople had a full range of safety devices. They had relatively cheap products, such as mass messaging software, classroom panic buttons, surveillance cameras, intruder alarms, and metal detectors. They contended that these products, even though they were reasonably priced, were highly effective.

The businesspeople also had more expensive tech products. As examples, they had facial recognition software and remotely activated locks. They contended that these products provided enough extra security to justify their higher prices.

The businesspeople pitched their products to school administrators. They realized that the administrators had the responsibility for school safety. They realized that they also had the responsibility for allocating school safety funds.

The businesspeople pitched their products to one more important group—parents. They anticipated that the parents would exert pressure on the administrators about how to spend their school safety funds.

Skeptics

The parents in Tampa were fascinated by school safety tech. They were hopeful that it would keep their children secure. They were ready to shift their safety funds from personnel to tech.

The pro-tech parents realized that they would need allies. They easily identified like-minded businesspeople and school administrators. However, they still needed their governor and state legislators to support them. They expected the governor to be a particularly formidable adversary.

The governor was not supportive. He had called for SROs in all schools. He still wanted them there. He told the legislators that safety tech would be less effective than the SROs. He asked them to stand firmly with him on this issue. He was pleased when they agreed.

The governor then went to police officers. He knew that they had the greatest experience with crime prevention. He asked them who was best equipped to confront armed assailants in the schools. He was pleased when they stated that highly trained SROs should confront them.

The legislators, governor, and police were joined by the National Rifle Association. The members of this group did not approve of schools that were relying exclusively on safety devices. They identified numerous cases in which armed assailants had been able to evade these devices. They predicted that they would continue to evade them.

The NRA members wanted SROs in the schools. They believed that they provided the most effective protection for students. However, they were willing to settle for armed guardians or armed teachers.

ANSWERING QUESTIONS ABOUT COMPLEX CONSEQUENCES

Floridians made a proposal to expand the duration of DST. However, they were surprised by the resistance to it.

Tampa Bay residents proposed to expand the use of school safety tech. They also were surprised by the resistance.

The efforts to expand DST and school safety tech did not affect each other. Nonetheless, they had some similarities. After you answer the following questions, see if you discern those similarities.

Question 1: Why Did Floridians Support the Expansion of Daylight Savings Time?

Floridians wished to expand DST. They were convinced that this change would have economic, health, and lifestyle benefits.

How did different groups respond to Floridians? Focus on two groups: businesspeople and state legislators.

Did businesspeople have low confidence, moderate confidence, or high confidence in the way that the Floridians were behaving? How did state legislators feel? Explain the bases for your answers.

When answering these questions, as well as those that follow, you can rely on the information in this chapter. You also might rely on some of the sources that are identified in the references at the back of the book. If you are reading this chapter with colleagues, you are encouraged to converse with them about the best way to answer the questions.

Question 2: Why Did the Department of Transportation Oppose the Expansion of Daylight Savings Time?

The staff at the federal Department of Transportation opposed Florida's proposal to expand DST. They insisted that the change would have troublesome consequences for interstate commerce. They supported half-year DST instead.

How did different groups respond to the staff at the Department of Transportation? Focus on two groups: businesspeople and state legislators.

Did businesspeople have low confidence, moderate confidence, or high confidence in the way that the staff was behaving? How did state legislators feel? Explain the bases for your answers.

Question 3: Why Did Tampa Bay Residents Support the Expansion of School Safety Tech?

Tampa Bay area residents wished to expand school safety tech. They were convinced that the change would protect students, teachers, and staff.

How did different groups respond to these residents? Focus on two groups: businesspeople and state legislators.

Did businesspeople have low confidence, moderate confidence, or high confidence in the way that the Tampa Bay residents were behaving? How did state legislators feel? Explain the bases for your answers.

Question 4: Why Did Florida's Governor Oppose the Expansion of School Safety Tech?

The governor rejected Tampa Bay's proposal to expand school safety tech. He insisted that the change would have too many troublesome consequences. He supported armed officers instead.

How did different groups respond to the governor? Focus on two groups: businesspeople and state legislators.

Did businesspeople have low confidence, moderate confidence, or high confidence in the way that the governor was behaving? How did state legislators feel? Explain the bases for your answers.

SUMMARY

Floridians wished to expand DST. They also wished to expand school safety tech. In both instances, they underestimated the resistance to these changes.

SEVEN

Do Parents in Roselle, Illinois, Have the Right Idea about School Tech?

> Violent video game play is associated with ... physical aggression.
> —Psychology Professor Jay Hull, 2018

> [The school shooting suspect played video games in which he'd] kill, kill, kill, blow up something, and kill some more, all day.
> —Suspect's Neighbor Paul Gold, 2018

> [The Illinois judge banned a] 16-year-old from violent video games [because he made a] school shooting threat.
> —Journalist James Batchelor, 2018

> I hope [the Illinois judge also bans the 16-year-old] from reading violent books, watching violent movies, and thinking violent thoughts.
> —Unidentified Blogger, 2018

Post office supervisors hoped to reduce workplace violence. They therefore distributed information about mental illness. However, they disappointed federal personnel, who replaced this plan with their own.

Educational administrators hoped to reduce school violence. They therefore installed video game–blocking filters on school computers. However, they disappointed an Illinois judge, who replaced their plan with his own.

POST OFFICE VIOLENCE

Employees had difficulty handling stressful jobs. Some of them became so frustrated that they attacked their supervisors and coworkers.

Members of the public were aware of violent workers. Some had learned about them from their own experiences. Others had learned from media accounts, such as those about an Oklahoma postal worker.

Patrick Sherrill was a postal worker who attracted enormous media attention during the 1980s. He entered the facility where he was employed, locked all of the doors, unpacked a gun, and attacked his fellow workers. He killed fourteen of them and wounded another six.

Journalists presented detailed accounts about Sherrill. They followed with explicit details about other violent mail workers. Coining a clever phrase, they wrote that all of these workers had *gone postal*.

Enthusiasts

Journalists at the *New York Times* identified ten postal employees who committed workplace murders from the late 1980s through the early 1990s. They were interested in the factors that had driven them to commit these crimes.

The journalists concluded that the postal workers had been subjected to "a treadmill of angry monotony . . . a minefield of festering grievances . . . [and] a boot camp, where supervisors behave like drill sergeants." They concluded that these conditions had driven them "over the edge."

Post office supervisors were under pressure to suppress workplace violence. However, they were not sure of the steps that they should take. They asked their senior administrators for advice.

The administrators believed that all of the assailants had been mentally ill. They therefore directed the supervisors to distribute information about the signs of this illness.

The administrators did provide this information. They then wondered whether it was having an impact. They kept their eyes on their workers, whom they hoped would display less violence.

The administrators were disappointed when workers still became violent. They therefore resolved to expand their information campaign. They went to federal legislators and requested the money that they would need.

The legislators did not give the post office the money that the administrators had requested. They gave it to a different federal agency—the office for Workplace Environment Improvement (WEI). They directed its staff to come up with a new plan to curb post office violence.

The staff at WEI quickly crafted a plan. They required that post offices establish "threat-assessment teams." They directed the members of these teams to document worker-on-worker attacks. They also directed them to take steps to prevent future attacks.

Skeptics

Some persons believed that the WEI plan was sound. However, others were skeptical of it.

The skeptics questioned the need for threat-assessment teams at post offices. They doubted that workers at these facilities were particularly violent.

The skeptics were a heterogeneous group. They included sociologists, law enforcement professionals, and the risk analysts at insurance firms. They compiled data indicating that workplace violence was much less common in post offices than in schools, hospitals, and mental health facilities.

The postal employees agreed with the skeptics. They had never felt particularly vulnerable at work. For this reason, they had largely ignored the earlier mental illness campaign. For the same reason, they ignored the threat assessment teams.

SCHOOL VIOLENCE

Journalists reported extensively about post office violence. They had been gratified when readers and viewers became excited about it. They wondered whether they would be just as excited about violence in other locations. They turned their attention to schools.

The journalists found instances in which teachers, administrators, and school staff members attacked each other. However, they focused instead on cases where students had attacked other students.

The journalists created a profile of the student assailants. They noted that they had severe psychological problems. They added that they also were preoccupied with video games.

The journalists examined the types of video games that the assailants had played. They noted that they had preferred ones in which characters toted computer-generated weapons and killed computer-generated antagonists. They assumed that they had been prodded by these games to carry actual weapons and kill real-world antagonists.

The journalists called for bans on violent video games. Although they approved of at-home video game bans, they did not think that these would halt school shootings. They preferred a nationwide ban.

Executives from the video game industry opposed the nationwide ban. They argued that it was unnecessary because youths understood the difference between shooting computer-generated images and shooting real persons.

Although the executives were skeptical of a ban on video games, they had to deal with an aroused and anxious public. They eventually were ready to compromise. They came up with an alternative proposal.

The executives proposed a code to rate the violence in games. They established a special commission, the Entertainment Software Rating Board (ESRB), to develop a rating code.

The members of the ESRB used letters to signify the audiences for video games. They directed teenagers to play games that were rated T (Teen) but avoid any that were rated M (Mature).

Some parents were not impressed with the ESRB's code. They doubted that it would have much impact. They wanted a nationwide ban.

The activist parents tried to gather support for the national ban. However, they made little progress. They therefore called for school-wide bans.

Educational administrators wished to appease the activist parents. Many of them agreed to video game bans at their schools.

The administrators then informed their students about their bans. They warned that anyone who violated them would forfeit screen time at school computers.

Businesspeople were not impressed by the video game bans. They doubted that they would reduce video game play on school computers. They had a better plan.

The businesspeople had developed special software filters. They proposed to adapt them to restrict video games at school.

Enthusiasts

School administrators were under pressure to demonstrate their commitment to student safety. They were eager to purchase computer filters. Those in Illinois were especially eager.

The Illinois administrators installed filters on the computers in classrooms, media centers, and tech labs. They assured parents that students would cease playing video games. They added that they then would cease assaulting their classmates. They were pleased when some of the parents agreed with them.

The Illinois administrators had confidence that the filters would discourage dangerous students. Nonetheless, they still urged teachers to be on the lookout for troublesome individuals.

Teachers throughout Illinois were on alert. Those in Roselle, a community thirty miles from Chicago, were particularly vigilant. They knew exactly what to do when a sixteen-year-old high schooler threatened to bring a gun to school. They reported him to the police.

The high schooler was arrested and ordered to appear in court. During the legal proceedings, he acknowledged that he had made the threat. However, he insisted that he never had owned a gun or even handled one. He explained that he had made the threat only to get attention.

The judge doubted that the student was being forthright. He therefore asked him a pointed question. He wanted to know if he ever had played violent video games.

The student replied honestly. He stated that he played them regularly and enjoyed them a great deal.

The judge concluded that violent video games were affecting this student. He was sure that they had prodded him to make the gun threat. He suspected that they would prod him to follow through on it.

The judge told the student that he was willing to let him go free. He added that he was even willing to let him return to school. However, he demanded that he pledge to cease playing video games.

Skeptics

Skeptics did not believe that the persons who played video games were on the road to perdition. They noted that most of them were responsible, law abiding, and psychologically well adjusted.

Many educators sided with the skeptics. In fact, some of them had used video games in their classrooms to inspire academic learning, creativity, and social maturity. One of them reported that his students found the games addictive. He quickly added "in the best way possible."

Some educators arranged school-sponsored video game competitions. Referring to these competitions as esports, they organized them for high schoolers and middle schoolers. Some even organized them for elementary school–aged children.

Students agreed with the skeptics. They had dismissed the notion that video games prodded violence. They questioned the need for video game filters at their schools. Some of them circumvented the filters and used their school computers in the same manner as they had before the filters were installed.

DEALING WITH CAUSES AND CORRELATIONS

Post office supervisors wished to discourage workplace violence. They therefore distributed information about mental illness. However, they failed to placate federal personnel, who replaced their plan with another.

Educational administrators wished to discourage school violence. They therefore installed filters to block video games at school. However, they failed to placate an Illinois judge, who replaced this plan with his own.

The events at post offices and schools did not affect each other. Nonetheless, they had some similarities. After you answer the following questions, see if you discern those similarities.

48   Chapter 7

Question 1: How Did Postal Supervisors Try to Discourage Workplace Violence?

Post office supervisors wished to discourage workplace violence. Convinced that it was linked to mental illness, they distributed information about this illness.

How did different groups respond to the supervisors? Focus on two groups: federal legislators and postal workers.

Did the legislators have low confidence, moderate confidence, or high confidence in the way that the post office supervisors were behaving? How did the workers feel? Explain the bases for your answers.

When answering these questions, as well as those that follow, you can rely on the information in this chapter. You also might rely on some of the sources that are identified in the references at the back of the book. If you are reading this chapter with colleagues, you are encouraged to converse with them about the best way to answer the questions.

Question 2: How Did a Federal Agency Try to Discourage Workplace Violence?

The staff at the office for Workplace Environment Improvement were disappointed by the plan to distribute mental illness information. They concluded that it was not stopping post office violence. They preferred to organize threat assessment teams.

How did different groups respond to the WEI staff? Focus on two groups: federal legislators and postal workers.

Did the legislators have low confidence, moderate confidence, or high confidence in the way that the WEI staff was behaving? How did the workers feel? Explain the bases for your answers.

Question 3: How Did Educational Administrators Try to Discourage School Violence?

Educational administrators wished to discourage school violence. Convinced that it was linked to video games, they installed filters to block students from playing these games at school.

How did different groups respond to the educational administrators? Focus on two groups: parents and students.

Did the parents have low confidence, moderate confidence, or high confidence in the way that these educational administrators were behaving? How did students feel? Explain the bases for your answers.

Question 4: How Did an Illinois Judge Try to Discourage School Violence?

An Illinois judge was disappointed by the video game filters. He concluded that they were not stopping school violence. He preferred to ban individual students from playing video games.

How did different groups respond to this judge? Focus on two groups: parents and students.

Did the parents have low confidence, moderate confidence, or high confidence in the way that this judge was behaving? How did students feel? Explain the bases for your answers.

SUMMARY

Post office supervisors were distressed about workplace violence. They hoped to control it by distributing information about mental illness. However, they disappointed federal personnel, who intervened with their own plan.

Educational administrators were distressed about school violence. They hoped to control it by installing computer filters to block video games. However, they disappointed an Illinois judge, who intervened with his own plan.

EIGHT
Do Silicon Valley's Parents Have the Right Idea about School Tech?

[In our family] we limit how much technology our kids use.
—Apple CEO Steve Jobs, 2011

[I don't believe that] technology alone is the answer to transforming education.
—Microsoft CEO Satya Nadella, 2017

I am . . . surrounded by super techies . . . [who send their children to schools with] no computers in the classroom.
—Professor Sherry Turkle, 2017

[My child views her school laptop as] a toy in the classroom.
—Unidentified Parent, 2019

Restaurant executives wished to increase sales and customer traffic. They therefore added healthy foods to their menus. School administrators wished to increase their parental approval ratings. They therefore added tech activities to their curricula. However, both groups reversed their strategies after they discerned little impact.

EXPANDING . . . AND THEN REDUCING . . . HEALTHY MENU ITEMS

The top executives at Burger King took pride in the number of restaurants they had built. They beamed when they eventually had more than 17,000. They assumed that investors were equally pleased.

The investors were pleased with the way the executives had handled the expansion of restaurants. However, they were not pleased with the way that they had handled some of their other important responsibilities.

They scolded them for failing to hit performance targets in sales and customer traffic.

Journalists perked up when they learned about the feud between Burger King's executives and investors. They anticipated that their readers would be intrigued. They decided to gather more details. They went to the executives and asked them directly about sales and customer traffic.

The executives did not wish to provide the journalists with damaging information about their chain. At the same time, they did not wish to provide them with misleading information. They therefore were honest. They acknowledged that the chain's sales and customer traffic had been declining. However, they immediately added that they were developing an innovative plan to reverse these trends.

The executives were under pressure to disclose their plan. They turned to McDonald's, their largest competitor, for ideas. They noted that McDonald's had added more salads, fruits, yogurts, and other healthy foods to its menu.

The executives documented that the McDonald's strategy had increased sales and customer traffic. They therefore announced that they would be adding more healthy foods to their own menus.

After they had put their plan into action, the executives kept track of sales and customer traffic. They were disappointed when both measures continued to decline.

The executives did not give up. They decided to employ a different strategy. This time, they would use that on which their chain's founders had relied.

Burger King's founders had not been concerned about healthy food. They had concentrated instead on cheap, appetizing, and enormously sized portions. They had been rewarded with bountiful sales and long customer queues.

Enthusiasts

The Burger King executives had not completely abandoned their founders' philosophy. For example, they had continued to offer menu selections such as the *Bacon King Hamburger Sandwich*.

The *Bacon King Hamburger Sandwich* was cheap, appetizing, and huge. However, it was not particularly healthy. Even when unaccompanied by a soft drink and fries, it had 1,150 calories.

The executives regretted the recent emphasis on healthy food choices at their restaurants. They feared that this emphasis had made their longtime customers view the *Bacon King Hamburger Sandwich* as an anomaly. As a result, it had compounded the damage caused by those healthy choices.

The executives wished to change the views of any longtime customers whom they had disappointed. They were going to get their attention by introducing a new item that was comparable to their mammoth *Bacon King Hamburger Sandwich*.

The executives had to revise their current menu to make room for the new item. They wished to keep the menu compact so that the items on it could be prepared quickly.

The executives were not going to have any difficulty eliminating a menu item. However, they had to identify the right item to replace it. They wanted that new item to appeal to their faithful customers.

The executives finally selected grilled hot dogs as their new menu item. They suspected that their customers would show the same gusto for hot dogs that they were showing for hamburgers.

The executives must have been pleased after they introduced the hot dogs and looked at consumer blogs for comments about them. One patron expressed excitement because he had been going to Burger King for burgers "and now they have dogs too."

The executives also searched for comments from business journalists. They knew that they were on the lookout for any changes at fast food restaurants. They anticipated that they would be interested in the hot dogs and then provide free publicity.

One journalist was quite impressed by the hot dogs. He wrote that their "flavor shined through the toppings" and that they taste "just like something you'd grill in your backyard." He then added that you "can't really beat the $1.99 price."

Skeptics

The executives had been excited about hot dogs. They had expected patrons to be equally excited. They smiled when some were.

Not all patrons were excited about the hot dogs. Some disapproved of them because of their ingredients. Others disapproved of them because of their flavor. They expressed their views on consumer blogs.

Journalists tended to agree with the skeptical patrons. One of them wrote a review with the title *Burger King's Hot Dogs Are a Disgusting Disgrace*. Another chose the title *I Might Be Dead by the Weekend*.

Burger King executives were confused by the comments about their hot dogs. They noted that some were extremely positive, while others were undeniably negative.

The executives decided to gather additional data. They were under pressure to increase sales and customer traffic at their restaurants. They therefore assessed these two key measures. They were disappointed when both of them continued to decrease.

The executives gathered data about one more measure. They looked at the number of competitors who were removing healthy foods from their menus and substituting hot dogs. They assumed that these competitors would be signaling confidence in the Burger King strategy. However, they failed to detect even one.

EXPANDING... AND THEN REDUCING... SCHOOL TECH

Persons who lived in the Silicon Valley felt fortunate. They had plentiful jobs, efficient civic services, premiere health care, top-notch dining, verdurous parks, low crime, ideal weather, attractive neighborhoods, and excellent education.

The administrators at Silicon Valley schools also felt fortunate. They worked in districts that had modern buildings, top-of-the-line equipment, master teachers, and academically talented students.

The school administrators felt fortunate for another reason: they worked with parents who appreciated their efforts and provided them with profuse praise. Although they valued this appreciation and praise, they wished to boost their approval ratings even higher.

The administrators believed that the best way to boost ratings would be to convince parents that their schools were truly outstanding. They looked at professional colleagues in other communities to see what strategies they had used to make this point. They noted that most of them had touted their exemplary school tech. They decided to copy them.

Numerous educational administrators in the Silicon Valley bragged about their commitment to tech. Nonetheless, those at a local high school were the most assertive. They stated that their commitment was demonstrated by their online courses, which had been adopted by schools in other states and even in other countries.

Most Silicon Valley administrators added more tech activities to their schools. However, some were disappointed when they then did not discern an increase in parental approval ratings.

The disappointed administrators looked for a different way to win over parents. They decided to employ a contrarian strategy: they were going to remove the tech activities and substitute something else.

Enthusiasts

The administrators had to explain to parents why they were removing tech activities. They realized that they would need help to make this point. They expected journalists to aid them.

Journalists were eager to help. They pointed out that almost all high schoolers had personal smartphones, tablets, or laptops. They noted that many middle schoolers and elementary schoolers had them as well. They did not think that they needed to be preoccupied with additional digital devices at school.

The anti-tech administrators had no trouble articulating reasons for dropping tech activities from curricula. However, they still had to specify the activities they would substitute.

Some of the anti-tech administrators were attracted to the learning activities of celebrated educators from a different era—Maria Montessori, John Dewey, and Rudolph Steiner. They announced that they would be substituting their learning activities for the tech activities. They then waited to see how parents would react.

Many Silicon Valley parents were excited. Those who worked at high-tech firms had already enveloped their children with digital devices. They saw no reason for the schools to envelop them even deeper.

Skeptics

Some parents were skeptical of the anti-tech schools. They conceded that they could be beneficial for children from affluent households. However, they doubted that they would be beneficial for children from poor households.

The skeptical parents identified highly reputable organizations that agreed with them. For example, they noted that the National School Boards Association had made school tech one of their highest priorities.

RESPONDING TO CONTRARIAN INITIATIVES

The executives at Burger King increased the number of healthy food items on their menus. However, they reversed course after they did not detect an increase in sales or customer traffic.

The administrators at Silicon Valley schools increased the number of tech activities in their curricula. However, they reversed course after they did not detect a gain in parent approval ratings.

The decisions made at Burger King restaurants and at Silicon Valley schools did not affect each other. Nonetheless, they had some similarities. After you answer the following questions, see if you discern any similarities.

Question 1: Why Did Restaurant Executives Add Healthy Items to Menus?

Executives at Burger King had relatively few healthy items on their menus. They added more to increase sales and customer traffic.

How did different groups respond to the executives who added healthy items to menus? Focus on two groups: fast food patrons and the leaders of competing fast food restaurants.

Did the patrons have low confidence, moderate confidence, or high confidence in the way that the Burger King leaders were behaving? How did the leaders of competing restaurants feel? Explain the bases for your answers.

When answering these questions, as well as those that follow, you can rely on the information in this chapter. You also might rely on some of the sources that are identified in the references at the back of the book. If you are reading this chapter with colleagues, you can converse with them about the best way to answer the questions.

Question 2: Why Did Restaurant Executives Drop Healthy Items from Menus?

Executives at Burger King were disappointed after healthy items did not increase sales or customer traffic. They therefore dropped some of them from their menus and substituted hot dogs.

How did different groups respond to the executives who dropped healthy items from menus? Focus on two groups: fast food patrons and the leaders of competing fast food restaurants.

Did the patrons have low confidence, moderate confidence, or high confidence in the way that the Burger King leaders were behaving? How did the leaders of competing restaurants feel? Explain the bases for your answers.

Question 3: Why Did School Administrators in the Silicon Valley Add Tech Activities to Curricula?

School administrators in the Silicon Valley had relatively few tech activities in their curricula. They added more to raise parental approval ratings.

How did different groups respond to the administrators who added tech activities? Focus on two groups: parents and the leaders of competing schools.

Did the parents have low confidence, moderate confidence, or high confidence in the way that these school administrators were behaving? How did the leaders of competing schools feel? Explain the bases for your answers.

Question 4: Why Did School Administrators in the Silicon Valley Drop Tech Activities from Curricula?

School administrators in the Silicon Valley were disappointed after tech activities did not raise parental approval ratings. They therefore dropped them from their curricula and substituted non-tech activities.

How did different groups respond to the administrators who dropped tech activities? Focus on two groups: parents and the leaders of competing schools.

Did the parents have low confidence, moderate confidence, or high confidence in the way that these school administrators were behaving? How did the leaders of competing schools feel? Explain the bases for your answers.

SUMMARY

Burger King's executives believed that they would benefit by adding healthy items to their menus. Silicon Valley's school administrators believed that they would benefit by adding tech activities to their curricula. However, both groups changed their minds after they detected few benefits.

NINE

Do New York City's Parents Have the Right Idea about School Tech?

> Computer-based testing [in this state will improve] . . . test delivery, test integrity, scoring validity, and turn-around time on testing results.
> —New York State Department of Education, 2019

> [This state's computer-based testing has] deteriorated into a chaotic, stressful situation.
> —New York State United Teachers, 2019

> The problems [we are having with computer-based testing are so extensive that they] . . . lead us to doubt that the state's current testing vendor . . . can ever produce acceptable results.
> —New York State Council of Superintendents President Bob Lowry, 2019

> Our children . . . will not take state-mandated [computer-based] tests.
> —New York City Parents Jeff Nichols & Anne Stone, 2018

Law school graduates detected irregularities in their bar exams. New York City parents detected them in their children's computerized exams. Both groups highlighted the harmful effects.

PROBLEMATIC BAR EXAMS

Law school students were eager to earn their degrees. They knew that they then would have to take and pass their bar exams before they could practice their profession.

After they had passed their bar exams, the graduates were optimistic about finding jobs. They had been assured that they would have no difficulty.

The graduates of 2011 were shocked when they looked for jobs. They found that relatively few were available. They went back to the administrators who had recruited them. They reminded them of the promises that they had made about a robust job market.

The law school administrators were caught off guard by the downturn in the job market. They told their graduates that they would investigate it.

The administrators discovered that large legal firms were depending less on their graduates and more on cheap overseas legal personnel. They concluded that the firms had created the employment problem through their outsourcing practices.

The graduates were not appeased by this explanation. They believed that the law school administrators themselves were to blame. They noted that they had been lowering admission standards at their schools to recruit ever larger classes. They accused them of creating a glut of lawyers.

The graduates wished to bolster this accusation with facts. They therefore began to monitor how many persons were taking bar exams. They also monitored how many were passing.

The graduates soon detected a curious pattern. Although the number of persons taking bar exams had been increasing, the number failing them also had been increasing. For example, over 4,800 persons took one of California's biannual bar exams in 2014; 47 percent of them failed. Two years later, over 5,200 persons took that exam and 63 percent failed. Four years later, over 5,300 persons took it and 70 percent failed.

The persons who failed the bar exam were upset because they could not compete for any jobs. However, they were upset for an additional reason: they believed that the score required to pass the exam had been manipulated to reduce the number of unemployed lawyers in the job market.

The failed-exam graduates contacted the administrators at their law schools. They wanted them to use their influence to lower the minimum score required for passing the bar exams. They were disappointed when the administrators showed little interest.

The failed-exam graduates wondered why the administrators did not wish to lower the scores. They concluded that the administrators were worried that the pool of unemployed lawyers would grow larger. They reasoned that they then would have a harder time attracting new students.

The graduates went to the American Bar Association (ABA). They complained that the law schools had conspired to set higher scores on the bar exams so that more students would fail. They suggested that the ABA revoke accreditation from any school at which more than 25 percent of the graduates were failing their bar exams.

Enthusiasts

The disgruntled graduates wanted a showdown at the 2017 ABA convention. They were delighted when some of the delegates agreed to help them. They asked them to introduce a resolution linking accreditation to passing rates on bar exams.

The graduates were pleased that they would have sympathetic delegates at the ABA convention. However, they realized that the law school administrators also would be present. They expected them to be formidable adversaries. They anticipated that they would need additional allies.

The graduates went to journalists. They asked them to inform their readers about the employment problems in the legal profession. They urged them to underscore the role that the law school administrators had played in creating these problems.

The journalists were eager to assist the disgruntled graduates. They wrote about their frustration while trying to find jobs. They noted that their frustration had been compounded by self-centered law school administrators. They heartily supported the accreditation changes for which the graduates were pushing. Many of them predicted that the changes would be enacted during the 2017 convention.

Skeptics

The law school administrators conceded that their graduates had employment troubles. However, they refused to accept the blame.

The administrators pointed out that some of their schools had high numbers of failing students but also high numbers of minority students. They did not want to see any changes that would make it more difficult for minority students to attend their schools.

Attorneys who were already licensed reviewed the current passing scores on bar exams. They did not want to see any changes to them. They may have had a selfish reason: lower scores would increase the number of persons competing for jobs in which the currently licensed attorneys were interested.

PROBLEMATIC SCHOOL EXAMS

New Yorkers paid attention to their children's school exams. They noted that some of them were designated by teachers, while others were designated by the state Department of Education.

The New Yorkers had a particular interest in the exams from the Department of Education. They realized that they had far-reaching consequences for their children and the schools in which they were enrolled.

The New York State Commissioner of Education headed the state Department of Education. This person had the responsibility for the state exams.

MaryEllen Elia was appointed as State Commissioner of Education in 2015. She was ready to make substantive changes to the state's assessment practices. She announced that she would be retiring printed tests and replacing them with computer-based tests (CBTs).

After Elia had made this announcement, she braced for a barrage of questions. She anticipated that parents would pose most of them. She was correct.

Parents asked how the schools were preparing for the CBTs. They wanted to know if they had CBT-compatible computers, high-speed internet access, the technical staff to support CBT sessions, and hacker-proof sites at which to store results.

Elia listened patiently to the parents. She acknowledged that the transition to CBTs might present some problems. However, she assured them that the CBTs themselves would have fewer problems than the tests they were replacing.

Elia had hoped to calm the anxious parents. However, she realized from their continued questions that she had not succeeded. She therefore made a concession. She would not require any schools to switch to CBTs during the first year of the rollout. She would leave that decision to principals.

Although Elia was concerned about the parents in every community, she was especially concerned about those in New York City. She knew that they had a history of carefully questioning state-mandated scholastic changes. She was anxious to see how they would respond to the CBTs.

Some of the New York City parents were concerned about the CBTs. They did not think their schools were ready for the change. They were not mollified by Elia's decision to let principals make the final decisions about using CBTs. They noted that some had made their decisions without consulting parents.

The parents predicted that the CBTs would have numerous practical problems. However, they had to wait for data from the State Department of Education to see whether this prediction was correct. In the meantime, they interviewed the teachers and students who had used the CBTs.

Enthusiasts

Commissioner Elia had anticipated that some parents in New York City would challenge the CBTs. She even had anticipated the strategy that they would employ: they would find weaknesses in the CBTs, enlist sympathetic journalists, and launch a coordinated attack.

The anti-CBT group did comprise parents and journalists. However, it also included teachers. The teachers were annoyed because Elia wished to make them responsible when students received low scores on CBTs.

Although Elia was prepared for resistors, she was confident that she would have supporters. She was counting on the support of the powerful businesspeople who marketed CBTs and the politicians who promoted them.

Elia also was counting on support from school administrators. She believed that some of them would use CBTs as a pretext for acquiring more tech funding.

Elia expected support from parents. She was confident that some of them shared her views about the need for more school tech, including CBTs.

Skeptics

The New York City students who took CBTs reported problems. They were extremely candid. They noted that their computers had crashed during testing sessions and that their teachers could not fix them.

The parents were upset because CBT scores had been compromised by shortages of reliable equipment and trained support staff. They were further upset after they learned that they had been tabulated with faulty software and stored at nonsecure sites.

The parents expressed their concerns to Commissioner Elia. They told her that they did not have confidence in the validity, safety, reliability, or efficiency of CBTs.

Elia tried to placate the parents. She agreed to increase the length of CBT testing sessions whenever computers or software malfunctioned. She also agreed to contact the CBT vendors and emphasize the importance of accurately calculating and securely protecting students' scores.

The parents were not satisfied. They were convinced that Elia was misleading them. They asked the New York State Board of Education to censure her.

The board ignored the request from the parents. Its members stood behind their commissioner. They also stood behind her decision to use CBTs.

The parents went to New York Governor Andrew Cuomo. They knew that he had appointed Elia. They urged him to admit that he had made an error, fire her, and halt the use of CBTs. They were disappointed when he backed his commissioner and the CBTs.

The parents had failed to get action from the State Board of Education and the governor. They therefore went to teachers, superintendents, jour-

64   Chapter 9

nalists, and the public. They asked them to support their efforts to remove CBTs from classrooms.

POSING QUESTIONS ABOUT CONTROVERSIAL ASSESSMENT

Law school graduates dutifully took their bar exams. However, they began to complain after they discovered irregularities in them.

New York City parents allowed their children to dutifully take state-mandated scholastic tests. However, they began to complain about the computerized versions after they discovered irregularities in them.

The events in law schools and those in public schools did not affect each other. Nonetheless, they had some similarities. After you answer the following questions, see if you discern any similarities.

Question 1: Why Did Law School Graduates Agree to Bar Exams?

Law school graduates realized that they were required to take bar exams. They agreed to take them in order to advance their legal careers.

How did different groups respond to the graduates who were dutifully taking bar exams? Focus on two groups: administrators at law schools and members of the American Bar Association.

Did the administrators have low confidence, moderate confidence, or high confidence in the way that the law school graduates were behaving? What about members of the American Bar Association—how did they feel? Explain the bases for your answers.

When answering these questions, as well as those that follow, you can rely on the information in this chapter. You also might rely on some of the sources that are identified in the references at the back of the book. If you are reading this chapter with colleagues, you are encouraged to converse with them about the best way to answer the questions.

Question 2: Why Did Law School Graduates Complain about Bar Exams?

Law school graduates noted an irregularity in their bar exams: the chances of getting passing scores on them grew smaller when the pool of unemployed lawyers was large. They complained about the harmful effects.

How did different groups respond to the graduates who complained about irregularities in their bar exams? Focus on two groups: administrators at law schools and members of the American Bar Association.

Did the administrators have low confidence, moderate confidence, or high confidence in the way that the law school graduates were behaving? What about members of the American Bar Association—how did they feel? Explain the bases for your answers.

Question 3: Why Did Parents in New York City Agree to the Printed Versions of State Tests?

Parents in New York City realized that their children were required to take state-prescribed tests. They agreed to let their children take the printed versions in order to advance their educations.

How did different groups respond to the parents who allowed children to dutifully complete the printed tests? Focus on two parties: teachers in the New York City schools and the State Commissioner of Education.

Did the teachers have low confidence, moderate confidence, or high confidence in the way that these parents were behaving? What about the State Commissioner of Education—how did she feel? Explain the bases for your answers.

Question 4: Why Did Parents in New York City Complain about the Computerized Versions of State Tests?

Parents in New York City noted irregularities in the state-prescribed tests: the equipment, supervisory personnel, scoring, and data storage required for the computerized versions were inadequate. They complained about the harmful effects.

How did different groups respond to the parents who complained about irregularities in their children's computerized tests? Focus on two parties: teachers in the New York City schools and the State Commissioner of Education.

Did the teachers have low confidence, moderate confidence, or high confidence in the way that these parents were behaving? What about the State Commissioner of Education—how did she feel? Explain the bases for your answers.

SUMMARY

Law school graduates detected irregularities in their bar exams. New York City parents detected them in their children's scholastic CBTs. Both groups highlighted the harmful effects.

TEN

Do Salt Lakers Have the Right Idea about School Tech?

> The average cost for a child to attend a year [of commercial] preschool in Utah is $8,052.
> —Journalist Becky Wright, 2016

> [Utah has a state-subsidized online preschool that can] prepare your preschooler for kindergarten at home.
> —Waterford Institute, 2018

> [Utah's online preschool] is far cheaper than traditional preschool.
> —Journalist Emma Brown, 2015

> The [average] price [for our online preschool] is $725.
> — Utah State Board of Education, 2016

Families in Salt Lake City worried about the high cost of commercial childcare and commercial preschool. They were drawn to less expensive alternatives, such as free-range childcare and online preschool.

CHEAP CHILDCARE

Utahns reside in a state that comprises 84,000 square miles. Although they have multiple places to settle, most of them choose Salt Lake City. They are lured to this area by plentiful jobs, efficient public transportation, amazing recreational opportunities, and urban amenities.

Even though the Salt Lakers resided in a nearly ideal community, they were anxious. They were especially anxious about their meager incomes.

Two adults maintained full-time jobs in most of the city's households. If they had young children, they needed someone to care for them.

The parents could have taken their children to one of the commercial childcare centers in Salt Lake City. However, many could not afford the fees. They repeatedly had asked their state legislators to help them.

The legislators recognized the parents' plight. They assured them that they would like to cover the cost of commercial childcare. Nonetheless, they judged that the amount required was too high.

The legislators worried about a backlash from the parents whom they did not assist. They were relieved when some of them stated that they no longer needed that assistance because they had adopted a novel childrearing philosophy—free-range childcare.

The free-range parents explained that they had been raised without adult supervision and then turned out well. In fact, they insisted that they were more independent, creative, and emotionally secure because of those early experiences. They were ready to raise their own children in the same manner.

Enthusiasts

The legislators were intrigued by free-range childcare. They liked the fact that it had no cost associated with it. Nonetheless, they worried that the parents who practiced it would be arrested for child negligence.

The legislators wished to demonstrate their support for the free-range parents. They anticipated that this support would endear them to these parents and also provide a rationale for their failure to fund traditional childcare.

The legislators set to work on a childcare law in 2018. They stipulated that those parents who practiced free-range childcare were protected from child-negligence charges. They beamed after the governor approved the bill.

Skeptics

The legislators waited to see the reaction to the law. They were interested in the reaction from parents.

The new childcare law was popular with the free-range parents. It reduced any guilt that they might feel for leaving their children unsupervised. It also reduced the chances that they might be charged with child negligence.

Dual-career parents felt differently about the new childcare law. They were skeptical of it. They noted that it did nothing for them because their children needed adult-supervised care.

The legislators were genuinely interested in how parents were responding to the new law. However, they knew that parents were influenced by journalists. They therefore wanted to know how the journalists were reacting.

The journalists had mixed reactions. Some of them had been publicly mocking those parents who were excessively cautious with their children. They encouraged them to consider free-range childcare as an alternative.

Although some journalists supported free-range childcare, others were skeptical. The skeptics doubted that it would prove to be as safe or beneficial as traditional, adult-supervised childcare. They suspected that the persons promoting it had ulterior motives.

CHEAP PRESCHOOL EDUCATION

Utah's state legislators were renowned for their frugality. They were pleased with the results. For example, they issued state bonds that were assigned *triple A* credit ratings.

The legislators in neighboring states were impressed by the skillful manner in which the Utahans had handled budgeting. They wondered whether they had handled education with comparable skill.

Utah's legislators had been quite successful with public education. Their state educational system regularly was ranked among the top ten in the nation.

No one doubted that Utah's public education system was excellent. Nonetheless, some persons questioned whether the state's legislators deserved the credit. The critics believed that the educational system had been influenced by some of Utah's notable assets. These assets included a low crime rate, strong economy, sound employment base, enviable health care, and modern infrastructure.

Although Utah had some eye-popping assets, it had some notable liabilities. These liabilities included its low population, marginal domestic product, and lagging household incomes.

Critics acknowledged that legislators had shown fiscal restraint when creating budgets. Nonetheless, they believed that they had shown too much restraint when creating their educational budgets.

The Salt Lakers were the loudest critics. They noted that their city's educational budget was far less than those of comparably sized cities. They wanted additional dollars. They gave an example of how they would use them: they intended to establish free, publicly funded preschools.

The state legislators recognized that their constituents prized preschooling. They also recognized that many of them could not afford to send their children to commercial preschools. They promised to address this problem during the 2016 legislative session.

Enthusiasts

The legislators investigated the annual cost of commercial preschooling in their state. They discovered that it was more than $8,000 per child. They asked the preschool operators if they were setting their rates too high.

The operators rejoined that their rates were reasonable. They pointed out that they were thousands of dollars less than in neighboring states. They suggested that families struggled to pay them because of their low household incomes.

The legislators agreed with the operators. They concluded that many families could not afford even reasonably priced preschools. They looked for a way to help them. They contacted the staff at the Waterford Institute, a nonprofit educational organization.

This institute's staff members were eager to get involved. They told the legislators that they could create a statewide preschool. However, they would have to make it available online in order to keep down the expenses.

The legislators were pleased with the proposal for the online preschool. They came up with a cumbersome name for it—*Utah Preparing Students Today for a Rewarding Tomorrow*. They encouraged persons to simply refer to it by its acronym: UPSTART.

The total annual cost to maintain *UPSTART* was less than $3 million. One reason that it was so modest was that subscribers would have to access it online. Another reason was that they would have to pay some of its cost.

The legislators pledged to keep the tuition reasonable. They set it at less than a thousand dollars per year. They then waited to see how parents would respond.

Parents were able to access *UPSTART* on their home computers and sample the lessons. They were satisfied with them. They also were satisfied with the amount of tuition they would have to pay for them.

Even though the legislators had made the tuition reasonable, they were worried that low-income parents would still be unable to pay it. They therefore gave them tuition waivers. They also gave them complimentary computers and free internet access.

Skeptics

Some parents who enrolled their children in *UPSTART* were pleased. They wrote testimonials about the enthusiasm that their children displayed and the academic gains that they made.

Other parents were disappointed. Dual-career parents were especially disappointed. They explained that they could only occasionally use *UP-*

START because it did not have live teachers to supervise and care for their children.

Some parents had an additional reason to question the online preschool. They noted that it did not give their children opportunities to interact with classmates and develop essential social skills.

Hispanic parents had one more reason to question the online preschool. Participants were required to disclose their residences and workplaces. They worried that this information would be used to prosecute undocumented immigrants.

POSING QUESTIONS ABOUT INEXPENSIVE PROGRAMS

Salt Lakers were upset about the high cost of commercial childcare. They looked for an inexpensive alternative. They adopted free-range childcare, which did not have any costs.

Salt Lakers also were upset about the high cost of commercial preschool. They once again looked for a low-cost alternative. They enrolled their children in the state-subsidized online preschool, which had few if any costs.

The behaviors that persons displayed when making decisions about childcare and preschool may not have affected each other. Nonetheless, they had some similarities. After you answer the following questions, see if you discern those similarities.

Question 1: Why Did Salt Lakers Subscribe to Commercial Childcare?

Salt Lakers sent their children to commercial childcare centers. They were convinced that they provided worthwhile care.

How did different groups respond to the Salt Lakers who subscribed to commercial childcare centers? Focus on two groups: state legislators and dual-career parents.

Did the legislators have low confidence, moderate confidence, or high confidence in the way that these Salt Lakers were behaving? How did dual-career parents feel? Explain the bases for your answers.

When answering these questions, as well as those that follow, you can rely on the information in this chapter. You also might rely on some of the sources that are identified in the references at the back of the book. If you are reading this chapter with colleagues, you are encouraged to converse with them about the best way to answer the questions.

Question 2: Why Did Salt Lakers Turn to Free-Range Childcare?

Some Salt Lakers subscribed to free-range childcare. They preferred it because it was less costly than commercial childcare.

How did different groups respond to the Salt Lakers who subscribed to free-range childcare? Focus on two groups: state legislators and dual-career parents.

Did the legislators have low confidence, moderate confidence, or high confidence in the way that these Salt Lakers were behaving? How did dual-career parents feel? Explain the bases for your answers.

Question 3: Why Did Salt Lakers Subscribe to Commercial Preschool?

Salt Lakers sent their children to commercial preschools. They were convinced that they provided worthwhile education.

How did different groups respond to the Salt Lakers who subscribed to commercial preschools? Focus on two groups: state legislators and dual-career parents.

Did the legislators have low confidence, moderate confidence, or high confidence in the way that these Salt Lakers were behaving? How did dual-career parents feel? Explain the bases for your answers.

Question 4: Why Did Salt Lakers Turn to Online Preschool?

Some Salt Lakers sent their children to Utah's online preschool. They preferred it because it was less costly than commercial preschool.

How did different groups respond to the Salt Lakers who subscribed to the online preschool? Focus on two groups: state legislators and dual-career parents.

Did the legislators have low confidence, moderate confidence, or high confidence in the way that these Salt Lakers were behaving? How did dual-career parents feel? Explain the bases for your answers.

SUMMARY

Salt Lakers were concerned about the high cost of commercial childcare and preschool. They explored less expensive alternatives, including free-range childcare and state-subsidized online preschool.

ELEVEN
Do San Antonians Have the Right Idea about School Tech?

[Educators who track students with RFID chips can] spend more time on lessons instead of clerical tasks.
—Scholar Chip, 2019

[This district tracks students with RFID chips because] parents expect that we always know where their children are.
—San Antonio's Northside Independent School District, 2012

Tracking students with RFID chips is pretty lucrative.
—Chip Free Schools, 2012

Don't let schools chip your kids.
—California ACLU Technology Director Nicole Ozer, 2010

Florida's legislators wished to speed up hurricane evacuations. They therefore reconfigured two-way roads so that motorists could drive on both sides of them. San Antonio's school administrators wished to speed up student rollcalls. They therefore made students carry RFID chips so that they could be electronically tracked.

IMPROVING HURRICANE EVACUATION

Florida's legislators worried about dangerous winds and torrential rains during their six-month-long hurricane season. They were concerned about the safety of residents.

Although residents in every part of Florida could be in danger during hurricanes, those along its 1,300-mile coast were in the greatest danger. They frequently were ordered to leave their communities. They then had to load family members, pets, food, water, and essential belongings into vehicles and proceed to designated evacuation routes.

Once the motorists had reached their evacuation routes, they were not stress-free. Locked in bumper-to-bumper traffic, they realized that their journeys would take two, three, four, or five times longer than they had planned. They found it difficult to reach gas stations, restaurants, and rest stops.

Floridians complained to their legislators about the problems that they faced during emergency evacuations. They threatened to ignore the evacuation orders if these problems were not fixed.

The Floridians had a suggestion about how to fix their problems. They recommended the use of contraflow, a procedure that converted two-directional highways into single-direction routes.

Enthusiasts

The legislators were familiar with contraflow. In fact, they once had implemented it experimentally. However, they had been displeased and discarded it.

The legislators were under pressure to reexamine contraflow. They promised to consider it carefully during their next legislative session.

The legislators needed help. They reached out to the staff at the Florida Department of Transportation (FDOT). They wanted their advice about the benefits and liabilities of contraflow.

The personnel at FDOT reviewed details from the earlier experiments with this procedure. They also gathered data from other states that had used it. They were impressed. They stated that they would like to conduct additional experiments.

The state legislators drafted a contraflow bill in 2018. They made sure to provide funding for more contraflow experiments. They then forwarded it to Governor Rick Scott.

The legislators told Scott that their constituents were frustrated by hurricane traffic jams. They assured him that their contraflow bill would be popular with them. They added that it also would be popular with retailers who were distressed by the many residents who were leaving communities early to avoid traffic problems.

Skeptics

Governor Scott did not doubt that contraflow would be popular. Nonetheless, he was not ready to implement it. He wished to discuss it further with the FDOT officials.

The officials told Scott that contraflow had a significant benefit: it increased the speed of the traffic along evacuation routes. However, they acknowledged that it had a major drawback: it required the stationing of state troopers at every entrance and exit along those routes. They explained that the troopers, who were needed to reduce confusion, were unavailable for other problems.

The troopers strongly opposed contraflow. Paramedics, medical technicians, firefighters, and utility workers also opposed it. All of these groups discouraged the governor from reintroducing contraflow.

Scott had heard enough. He announced that he would not be implementing contraflow. In fact, he would not even be conducting any more experiments on it. He would come up with alternative ways to deal with hurricane traffic. He went back to the FDOT for assistance.

The FDOT officials had two suggestions to help evacuating motorists. They recommended that they drive on the shoulders of roads as well as in the major lanes. They also recommended that they zip through toll booths without stopping to pay.

Scott liked both of these suggestions. He acknowledged that they might not speed up traffic as much as contraflow. However, he was confident that they would be much safer.

The pro-contraflow group was disappointed with Scott. They were even more disappointed with their legislators, who changed their minds about contraflow and withdrew their support for it.

IMPROVING STUDENT MONITORING

The school administrators in San Antonio kept tabs on their students. At the high schools, they relied on daily rollcalls.

The administrators realized that rollcalls were cumbersome. However, they insisted that they were needed to confirm that students were present, learning, and safe.

The administrators had another reason to take rollcalls. They were the bases of the attendance reports that they forwarded to the state. These reports then influenced the amount of funding they received.

The administrators wished to ensure that their attendance reports were as accurate as possible. However, they also wished to ensure that they were completed quickly. They turned to businesspeople and asked whether they could assist.

The businesspeople were eager to give advice. They based it on their own efforts at monitoring merchandise. They explained that they had been attaching electromagnetic chips to items and then using digital devices to track their locations. They referred to this process as radio frequency identification (RFID).

The businesspeople explained that they had another use for RFID chips. They had been tracking employees by making them carry the chips. They urged the school administrators to track students in the same way.

The administrators in San Antonio's Northside School District were intrigued with RFID chips. They wondered how much they would have to spend on them. They were shocked when they discovered that they would need over a million dollars to supply all of their students with RFID chips.

The administrators wished to spend less. They purchased just enough RFID chips for the students at two high schools. Nonetheless, they still had to pay for the tracking devices, maintenance contracts, and service fees. Their total bill came to over half a million dollars.

Enthusiasts

The Northside school administrators bought the RFID chips and tracking equipment in 2012. They could not have been more excited. They hoped that key constituents would share their excitement. They wanted to hear from local businesspeople.

San Antonino's businesspeople had been using RFID chips for years. They were sure that they had saved money and improved efficiency. They predicted that the administrators would see similar results. They told them that they were supportive.

The administrators also were concerned about state legislators. They wondered how they would respond.

The legislators believed that too many students were skipping school. They had built attendance into Texas's educational funding formula to discourage truancy. They were confident that they RFID chips would help with this problem. They told the administrators that they were supportive.

The administrators were concerned about teachers. They assured them that the RFID chips would eliminate laborious rollcalls. They predicted that they then would have more time for instruction. They were grateful when some of them expressed support.

The administrators were concerned about one more group—parents. They worried that they might view RFID chips as too intrusive. They tried to win them over with an assurance that the chips would protect their children. They were pleased when some agreed.

Skeptics

Although some parents had confidence in the RFID chips, others did not. The skeptics suspected that the school administrators had a financial motive for purchasing them.

The skeptical parents discovered a report from the district's RFID vendor. In that report, the vendor had estimated that the district would see an enormous boost in state funding if it employed their technology. The vendor had predicted that this boost would be enough to pay for the technology and then leave $500,000 in additional revenue.

The skeptical parents had another reason for objecting to the RFID chips. They noted that the chips would provide information about all of their children's movements, including their visits to restrooms and the lengths of those visits. They doubted that the school administrators needed this information.

The parents urged the administrators to halt the RFID experiment. When they realized that they were not listening, they looked for another way to get their attention.

The members of one San Antonio family came up with a truly novel way to get attention. They were convinced that the RFID chips were connected to satanic rituals. They sued the administrators for coercing them to participate in the rituals.

The litigating family members received free media coverage from journalists. They then received free legal advice from civil liberties advocates. Although some of these parties may have questioned whether RFID chips had satanic links, they firmly believed that they should not be used without parental approval.

The Northside administrators had underestimated the opposition to the RFID chips. After they realized that they had made a mistake, they announced that they had changed their minds and would no longer be using them.

POSING QUESTIONS ABOUT UNUSUAL SOLUTIONS TO PROBLEMS

Florida's legislators wished to speedily evacuate residents during hurricanes. They came up with an unusual plan: they made motorists drive on both sides of two-way roads.

San Antonio's school administrators wished to rapidly monitor student attendance. They came up with an unusual plan: they made students carry RFID chips.

The behaviors that legislators displayed when making decisions about roads and those that school administrators displayed when making decisions about students did not affect each other. Nonetheless, they had some similarities. After you answer the following questions, see if you discern those similarities.

Question 1: Why Did Florida's Legislators Use Contraflow?

Florida's legislators required residents to evacuate during hurricanes. However, they realized that they were bogged down because they could drive on only one side of two-way roads. They used contraflow to speed up the process.

How did different groups respond to the legislators? Focus on two groups: evacuees and emergency responders.

Did the evacuees have low confidence, moderate confidence, or high confidence in the way that these legislators were behaving? How did the emergency responders feel? Explain the bases for your answers.

When answering these questions, as well as those that follow, you can rely on the information in this chapter. You also might rely on some of the sources that are identified in the references at the back of the book. If you are reading this chapter with colleagues, you are encouraged to converse with them about the best way to answer the questions.

Question 2: Why Did Florida's Legislators Abandon Contraflow?

Florida's legislators were confronted by critics who contended that contraflow compromised safety. When they were unable to appease them, they abandoned the procedure.

How did different groups respond to the legislators? Focus on two groups: evacuees and emergency responders.

Did the evacuees have low confidence, moderate confidence, or high confidence in the way that these legislators were behaving? How did the emergency responders feel? Explain the bases for your answers.

Question 3: Why Did School Administrators in San Antonio Use RFID Chips?

School administrators in San Antonio required teachers to monitor students' attendance. However, they realized that they were bogged down by laborious rollcalls. They used RFID chips to speed up the process.

How did different groups respond to these school administrators? Focus on two groups: parents and civil liberties advocates.

Did the parents have low confidence, moderate confidence, or high confidence in the way that these school administrators were behaving? How did the civil liberties advocates feel? Explain the bases for your answers.

Question 4: Why Did School Administrators in San Antonio Abandon RFID Chips?

San Antonio's school administrators were confronted by critics who contended that RFID chips compromised students' rights. When they were unable to appease them, they abandoned the chips.

How did different groups respond to these school administrators? Focus on two groups: parents and civil liberties advocates.

Did the parents have low confidence, moderate confidence, or high confidence in the way that these school administrators were behaving?

How did the civil liberties advocates feel? Explain the bases for your answers.

SUMMARY

Florida's legislators wished to speed up roadway evacuations during hurricanes. They turned to contraflow. However, critics demanded that they abandon the procedure because of unanticipated complications.

San Antonio's school administrators wished to speed up their daily rollcalls of student attendance. They turned to RFID chips. However, critics demanded that they abandon the procedure because of unanticipated complications.

TWELVE
Do Seattle's Parents Have the Right Idea about School Tech?

> Many students in the Seattle area . . . are given lifelike, robot babies that cry throughout the night.
> —Journalist Page Cornwell, 2016

> [Our firm's robot baby] cries . . . when shaken.
> —RealCare Shaken Baby, 2019

> [The robot babies are] designed to discourage teen pregnancy.
> —Journalist Leah Samuel, 2016

> The cure for teenage pregnancy is more difficult than a magic doll.
> —Obstetrics/Gynecology Professor Julie Quinlivan, 2016

School administrators tried to dissuade students from risky behavior. They used prison visits to discourage them from crime and robot babies to discourage them from premarital sex.

ANXIETY-ELICITING PRISON VISITS

School administrators knew that students would misbehave. They expected their teachers to handle them. However, they did not expect them to handle those who were violent.

The administrators realized that teachers needed help with violent students. They reached out to professionals in juvenile corrections. They knew that they had programs for youthful offenders. They asked if they could modify them for those youths who returned to school. They were excited when they agreed.

The administrators were generally pleased with the programs from the corrections personnel. They judged that they were helping teachers deal with students who had committed crimes. However, the teachers still needed help with the many students who were at risk for committing crimes.

The administrators wanted more advice. This time they went to mental health counselors. They explained that they needed preventive strategies.

The counselors were willing to help. They had developed clinical programs for emotionally and psychologically troubled youths. They were certain that they could fashion them into preventive programs for schools.

The programs that the mental health counselors developed required the cooperation of substance abuse specialists, community agency representatives, and law enforcement professionals. They were socially progressive, complicated, and expensive.

At the end of the 1970s, a group of convicts came up with a different sort of program for at-risk students. Their program was reactionary, simple, and cheap.

The convicts invited students to prison. They had a single goal: to make the students aware of the terrifying consequences of crime.

Enthusiasts

The prison visits would have gone unheralded had it not been for Arnold Shapiro. Shapiro was a talented filmmaker who recorded the visits and edited them into a documentary movie.

Shapiro was ready to release his movie to the public. However, he needed a catchy name for it. He wanted one that would encapsulate the motive for inviting youths to prison. He came up with the perfect title: *Scared Straight*.

The movie succeeded beyond all of Shapiro's expectations. It was enthusiastically reviewed, widely screened, and honored with an Academy Award.

Journalists, film critics, and cinema patrons were impressed with Shapiro's movie. School administrators also were impressed. The administrators had been searching for a low-cost way to prevent violent crime. They believed that they had found it: they would replicate the experiences that were chronicled in the movie.

Some administrators adapted the experiences in the movie. They made them even more frightening. For example, they sent students to morgues to view bullet-riddled corpses. Others sent them to corrections camps where they had to endure abuse. They were eager to see how the students reacted.

Skeptics

Students reacted emotionally to the scared straight visits. Many were psychologically scarred by them. They complained to their parents.

The parents went to the school administrators who had arranged the scared straight visits. They told them that their children found them disturbing. They made it clear that they shared their children's views.

The parents objected to scared straight visits for still another reason. They noted that these visits, which represented prisons as threats, were contrary to recent research. This research had demonstrated that these sorts of threats had not been effective deterrents for criminals.

The parents predicted that the scared straight visits would create more problems than they solved. Nonetheless, they had to wait until they had the data to confirm this prediction. After several years, they were ready to see if the participants had stayed out of trouble.

The participants in the scared straight visits had not avoided trouble. Quite to the contrary, they had been in trouble at a rate that was higher than that for nonparticipants.

ANXIETY-ELICITING ROBOT BABIES

The school administrators in Seattle knew that some of their students were sexually active. They were genuinely concerned about the physical, psychological, and emotional damage that they might sustain. They anticipated that this damage would be compounded if they became pregnant.

Even though the administrators were concerned about sexually active students, they had refused to get involved. They insisted that parents had this responsibility. They urged those parents who needed assistance to consult with religious leaders or medical professionals.

Some parents respected the administrators' stance on sex education. However, even they became alarmed when the number of births by students increased. They pleaded with the administrators to change their minds and get involved.

The administrators relented and agreed to provide sex instruction. However, they made it clear that they would provide only *risk-avoidance* instruction.

Risk-avoidance instruction presented students with simple and straightforward messages about sex. It informed them that sex placed them *at risk* for diseases and pregnancy. It directed them to *avoid* sex to eliminate these risks.

After the school administrators had commenced risk-avoidance instruction, they wondered how influential groups in the community were responding. They were concerned about religious leaders.

The religious leaders had assumed that sex instruction would backfire and actually increase the number of students who were sexually active. Although they preferred a total ban on it, they were willing to compromise and settle for risk-avoidance instruction.

The school administrators also were concerned about parents. They noted that many of them had approved of their original decision to avoid sex education. They wondered how they would react to their shift.

The parents who had objected to sex education looked to their religious leaders for guidance. When they realized that these leaders had agreed to risk-avoidance instruction, they also agreed to it.

The school administrators were excited by the reception from religious leaders and parents. However, they also kept their eyes on students.

The school administrators were disappointed when the students hardly paid any attention to risk-avoidance instruction. They became even more disappointed when they exhibited a rising rate of pregnancy.

The school administrators had no choice but to modify their sex education program. However, they were not sure how to proceed. They contacted professionals in the health fields for assistance.

The health professionals were eager to get involved. They had been experimenting with socially progressive sex education programs. They stated that they could adapt them for the schools. However, they noted that these programs, because they were comprehensive and complex, would require the cooperation of specialized personnel in health and social work.

Some of Seattle's school administrators were ready for socially progressive sex education programs. They assembled multidisciplinary teams to implement them.

Like the risk-avoidance program that they had replaced, the socially progressive programs informed students about abstinence. However, they gave them additional information about sexual anatomy, LGBT sex, birth control, consent, and the characteristics of healthy sexual relationships.

The school administrators were excited by the content in the socially progressive sexual education programs. They were even more excited by the results: the rate of teen pregnancy seemed to be declining. However, they were distressed by the difficulty—and the expense—of maintaining these programs. They therefore kept their eyes peeled for a simpler and cheaper alternative.

During the 1990s, the Seattle school administrators caught wind of novel, bargain-priced devices—robot babies. They wondered if these devices, which purported to reduce teen pregnancy, could be the panacea for which they had been searching.

Robot babies had similarities to the toy babies that were designed for young children. However, the robot babies were intended for teens, were wired to loud alarms, and required continual care to keep the alarms from screeching.

Enthusiasts

Seattle's school administrators purchased and distributed robot babies. They told their students that these electronic devices would teach them what it was like to care for an infant. They warned them to treat the devices as if they were living human beings.

When the school administrators were explaining robot babies to parents, they changed their tone. They confided that these intrusive and irritating devices had been designed to dissuade students from engaging in premarital sex and conceiving children.

Some parents had been devoted to the risk-avoidance programs. They had been frustrated after critics had linked these programs to an out-of-date philosophy. They noted that the robot babies, even though they were based on a similar philosophy, embodied the latest technology. They therefore were excited about them.

Skeptics

The parents who had liked the risk-avoidance programs liked the robot babies. However, those who had been skeptical of these programs were equally skeptical of the robots.

The skeptical parents disapproved of robot babies for another reason. They doubted that they would be effective. They were sure that their children could discern the difference between squealing electronic toys and genuinely distressed infants.

The skeptical parents predicted that teens who carried robot babies would be embarrassed and offended by them. They were correct.

The skeptical parents then made another prediction. They anticipated that teens who carried robot babies would not exhibit a lower rate of pregnancy.

The skeptical parents could not immediately confirm their second prediction. They had to wait until the teens had been given robot babies and lugged them about.

The skeptical parents eventually had the data they needed. They were not surprised that teens who participated in the robot baby program did not have an especially low rate of pregnancy. However, they were truly surprised that they actually had a higher rate than nonparticipants.

Journalists sensed that their audiences would be fascinated by the controversy over robot babies. They were eager to gather more details.

The journalists interviewed academic researchers who had studied robot babies. They quickly surmised that these researchers had no confidence in the devices.

The journalists then contacted the school administrators who had purchased robot babies. They asked for their reaction to the academic researchers. However, the administrators referred them to the manufacturers.

The journalists followed this suggestion and contacted the manufacturers. They asked for their reactions to the professors who had investigated robot babies.

A spokesperson for one firm listened to the journalists for a moment before she corrected them. She told them that they should refer to her firm's products as *infant simulators* rather than *robot babies*. She then added that they should refer to the professors who had attacked her firm as *junk scientists* rather than *academic researchers*.

POSING QUESTIONS ABOUT ANXIETY-ELICITING PROGRAMS

School administrators wished to deter students from crime. They also wished to deter them from premarital sex. In both cases, they experimented with programs that were socially progressive and expensive. They also experimented with programs that were less progressive and less expensive. They then compared the results.

The behaviors that school administrators displayed when respectively making decisions about crime and premarital sex may not have affected each other. Nonetheless, they had some similarities. After you answer the following questions, see if you discern those similarities.

Question 1: Why Did School Administrators Use Progressive Juvenile Justice Programs?

School administrators implemented socially progressive juvenile justice programs. They believed that they reduced the chances that students would commit crimes.

How did different groups respond to the school administrators who were implementing progressive juvenile justice programs? Focus on two groups: students and parents.

Did the students have low confidence, moderate confidence, or high confidence in the way that their school administrators were behaving? How did parents feel? Explain the bases for your answers.

When answering these questions, as well as those that follow, you can rely on the information in this chapter. You also might rely on some of the sources that are identified in the references at the back of the book. If you are reading this chapter with colleagues, you are encouraged to converse with them about the best way to answer the questions.

Question 2: Why Did School Administrators Turn to Scared Straight Programs?

The school administrators turned away from socially progressive juvenile justice programs. They concluded that they were simply too expensive. They substituted scared straight programs. They were sure that they would be less expensive. They hoped that they would be just as effective.

How did different groups respond to the school administrators who were implementing scared straight programs? Focus on two groups: students and parents.

Did the students have low confidence, moderate confidence, or high confidence in the way that their school administrators were behaving? How did parents feel? Explain the bases for your answers.

Question 3: Why Did School Administrators in Seattle Use Progressive Sex Education?

Administrators implemented socially progressive sex education in Seattle's schools. They believed that it reduced the chances that students would engage in premarital sex and become pregnant.

How did different groups respond to the administrators who were implementing progressive sex education? Focus on two groups: students and parents.

Did the students have low confidence, moderate confidence, or high confidence in the way that the administrators were behaving? How did parents feel? Explain the bases for your answers.

Question 4: Why Did School Administrators in Seattle Turn to Robot Babies?

Administrators turned away from socially progressive sex education in Seattle's schools. They concluded that it was simply too expensive. They substituted robot babies. They were sure that they would be less expensive. They hoped that they would be just as effective.

How did different groups respond to the administrators who relied on robot babies? Focus on two groups: students and parents.

Did the students have low confidence, moderate confidence, or high confidence in the way that the administrators were behaving? How did parents feel? Explain the bases for your answers.

SUMMARY

School administrators searched for ways to deter students from crime. They initially tried socially progressive juvenile justice programs. They later switched to prison visits.

The administrators also wished to deter students from premarital sex. They initially tried socially progressive sex education. However, they later switched to robot babies.

References

REFERENCES FOR *BEGINNING OF PREFACE QUOTES*

Flynn, A.—*quoted by* Richtel, M. (2011, October 23). "Silicon Valley school that doesn't compute." *New York Times*. Retrieved from: https://www.nytimes.com/2011/10/23/technology/at-waldorf-school-in-silicon-valley-technology-can-wait.html.

Microsoft Corporation. (2017, June 13). "The technology revolution transforming education." Retrieved from: https://news.microsoft.com/europe/2017/06/13/the-technology-revolution-transforming-education.

Moore, M.—*quoted by* Barseghian, T. (2012, March 6). "Students demand the right to use technology in schools." KQED.org. Retrieved from: https://www.kqed.org/mindshift/19649/students-demand-the-right-to-use-technology-in-schools.

Pierre-Louis, L. (2011, March 22). "Why every child should have a computer at an early age." Broadbandandsocialjustice.org. Retrieved from: http://broadbandandsocialjustice.org/2011/03/why-every-child-should-have-a-computer-at-an-early-age.

REFERENCES FOR CHAPTER 1

References for Beginning of Chapter 1 Quotes

Ashton, M. (2018, August 17). "Why I'm starting the first computer science middle school in Washington, DC." *USA Today*. Retrieved from: https://www.usatoday.com/story/opinion/2018/08/17/im-starting-first-computer-science-middle-school-washington-column/918062002.

Dolobowsky, B.—*quoted by* Cotroneo, N. (2007, March 11). "No textbooks, no resources, parents complain." *New York Times*. Retrieved from: https://www.nytimes.com/2007/03/11/nyregion/nyregionspecial2/11LImain.html.

English, C. (2015, August 20). "Parents, students want computer science education in school." Gallup.com. Retrieved from: https://news.gallup.com/poll/184637/parents-students-computer-science-education-school.aspx.

Jones, G. (2017, March 27). "5 Biggest barriers to education technology." Edudemic.com. Retrieved from: http://www.edudemic.com/barriers-to-education-technology.

References for Fat Shaming — Introduction

Aleccia, J. (2013, January 24). "Fat-shaming may curb obesity, bioethicist says." Today.com. Retrieved from: https://www.today.com/health/fat-shaming-may-curb-obesity-bioethicist-says-1C8095045.

Farrell, A. E. (2011). *Fat shame: Stigma and the fat body in American culture*. New York: New York University Press.

References for Fat Shaming — Enthusiasts

Aamodt, S. (2016). *Why diets make us fat: The unintended consequences of our obsession with weight loss*. New York: Current.

Adkins, S. (2016). *Cause related marketing*. New York: Routledge.

Callahan, D. (2013, January 1). "Obesity: Chasing an elusive epidemic." *Hastings Center Report*. Onlinelibrary.wiley.com. Retrieved from: https://onlinelibrary.wiley.com/doi/full/10.1002/hast.114.

Fine, S. H. (Ed.). (2017). *Marketing the public sector: Promoting the causes of public and nonprofit agencies*. New York: Routledge.

Greenhalgh, S. (2015). *Fat-talk nation: The human costs of America's war on fat*. Ithaca, NY: Cornell University Press.

Karolä, K. (2016). *The weight of images: Affect, body image and fat in the media*. New York: Routledge.

Northrop, J. M. (2014). *Reflecting on cosmetic surgery: Body image, shame and narcissism*. New York: Routledge.

Rice, R. E., & Atkin, C. K. (Eds.). (2017). *Public communication campaigns*. Thousand Oaks, CA: Sage.

Tanzi, A. (2018, December 20). "The average American is edging closer to being obese." Bloomberg.com. Retrieved from: https://www.bloomberg.com/news/articles/2018-12-20/tale-of-the-tape-average-american-is-borderline-obese-cdc-says.

US Department of Health and Human Services. (2000). *Reducing tobacco use: A report of the Surgeon General*. Washington, DC: Author.

Wand, K. (2012). *Tobacco and smoking: Opposing viewpoints*. Detroit, MI: Greenhaven.

References for Fat Shaming — Skeptics

Abrams, L. (2013, January 23). "A case for shaming obese people, tastefully." *Atlantic*. Retrieved from: https://www.theatlantic.com/health/archive/2013/01/a-case-for-shaming-obese-people-tastefully/267446/.

Czerniawski, A. M. (2015). *Fashioning fat: Inside plus-size modeling*. New York: New York University Press.

Farley, T. A. (2015, December 18). "The problem with focusing on childhood obesity." *New York Times*. Retrieved from: http://www.

nytimes.com/2015/12/18/opinion/the-problem-with-focusing-on-childhood-obesity.html.

Mendible, M. (2016). *American shame: Stigma and the body politic*. Bloomington: Indiana University Press.

Young, R. (2018, October 31). "Fat shame: Being overweight is often not a choice—being ashamed is." *Psychology Today*. Retrieved from: https://www.psychologytoday.com/us/blog/contemporary-psychoanalysis-in-action/201810/fat-shame.

References for Computer Shaming—Introduction

Bauerlein, M. (2011). *The digital divide: Arguments for and against Facebook, Google, texting, and the age of social networking*. New York: Penguin.

Dodge, D. (2017, September 16). "Is computer coding for kids a fad or an essential new literacy?" Codakid.com. Retrieved from: https://codakid.com/is-computer-coding-for-kids-a-fad-or-an-essential-new-literacy.

Geller, A., & Khosla, N. (2016, January 7). "Don't lose track of education technology in the new education law." *Forbes*. Retrieved from: https://www.forbes.com/sites/under30network/2016/01/07/dont-lose-track-of-education-technology-in-the-new-education-law/amp.

Lohr, S. (2018, December 4). "Digital divide is wider than we think, study says." *New York Times*. Retrieved from: https://www.nytimes.com/2018/12/04/technology/digital-divide-us-fcc-microsoft.html.

Straubhaar, J. D., Spencem, J., Tufekci, Z., & Lentz, R. G. (2013). *Inequity in the technopolis: Race, class, gender, and the digital divide in Austin*. Austin: University of Texas Press.

References for Computer Shaming—Enthusiasts

Ashworth, C. (2017, July 24). "Bridging the digital divide: How to stop technology leaving young people behind." *Guardian*. Retrieved from: https://www.theguardian.com/voluntary-sector-network/2017/jul/24/bridging-digital-divide-technology-youth-skills.

Computer Science Education Week Editors. (2018, December 3–9). "Sample email or letter to your school." Csedweek.org. Retrieved from: https://csedweek.org/promote/letter.

Erickson, E. (2017). "8 Reasons coding for kids isn't just another fad." Bitsbox.com. Retrieved from: https://bitsbox.com/blog/eight-reasons-coding-for-kids-isnt-just-another-fad.

Krueger, N. (2017, June 24). "Engaging parents as school tech leaders." International Society for Technology in Education. Retrieved from: https://www.iste.org/explore/articleDetail?articleid=1013.

Sparvell, M. (2018, August 29). "New survey: What parents think about technology in the classroom." Microsoft.com. Retrieved from:

https://educationblog.microsoft.com/2018/08/new-survey-what-parents-think-about-technology-in-the-classroom.

References for Computer Shaming—Skeptics

Blanken, L. (2014, May 29). "Coding is a fad." Geekymomblog.com. Retrieved from: http://www.geekymomblog.com/2014/05/coding-is-a-fad/.

Cronin, B. (2013, May 22). "Buying a computer won't raise your kids' grades." *Wall Street Journal*. Retrieved from: https://blogs.wsj.com/economics/2013/05/22/buying-a-computer-wont-raise-your-kids-grades.

Guzdial, M. (2014, May 28). "Adding coding to the curriculum: Considering the claims." Computinged.wordpress.com. Retrieved from: https://computinged.wordpress.com/2014/05/28/adding-coding-to-the-curriculum-considering-the-claims.

Herold, B. (2018, September 25). "Jobs at all levels now require digital literacy." *Education Week*. Retrieved from: https://www.edweek.org/ew/articles/2018/09/26/jobs-at-all-levels-now-require-digital.html.

Irvine, M. (2018, December 5). "Limiting screen time for your kid: It's harder than it looks. *Florida Times-Union*. Retrieved from: http://digital.olivesoftware.com/Olive/ODN/FloridaTimesUnion/shared/ShowArticle.aspx?doc=TFTU%2F2018%2F12%2F05&entity=Ar02901&sk=95FD0782&mode=text.

Johnson, K. (2000, June 14). "Do computers in the classroom boost academic achievement?" Heritage Foundation. Retrieved from: https://www.heritage.org/education/report/do-computers-the-classroom-boost-academic-achievement.

Ortutay, B. (2018, September 3). "From penny press to Snapchat: Parents fret through the ages." *Washington Post*. Retrieved from: https://www.washingtonpost.com/business/technology/from-penny-press-to-snapchat-parents-fret-through-the-ages/2018/09/03/ab3d98ca-af97-11e8-8b53-50116768e499_story.html.

Wente, M. (2017, August 15). "Coding for kids: Another silly fad." *Globe and Mail*. Retrieved from: https://www.theglobeandmail.com/opinion/coding-for-kids-another-silly-fad/article35982667/.

Winfield, A. (2017, September 20). "The coding for kids debate: Fundamental or fad?" *Forbes*. Retrieved from: https://www.forbes.com/sites/sap/2017/09/20/the-coding-for-kids-debate-fundamental-or-fad/#3901c4361c4c.

REFERENCES FOR CHAPTER 2

References for Beginning of Chapter 2 Quotes

Lapowsky, S. (2015, April 8). "What school." *Wired*. Retrieved from: https://www.wired.com/2015/05/los-angeles-edtech.

Magruder, S.—*quoted by* Gilbertson, A. (2014, August 25). "LA schools iPad project: How it started . . . before the bidding began." SCPR.org. Retrieved from: https://www.scpr.org/blogs/education/2014/08/25/17192/how-did-la-schools-decide-on-ipad-software-it-star.

Newcombe, T. (2015, May 13). "A cautionary tale for any government IT project: L.A.'s failed iPad program." Governing.com. Retrieved from: http://www.governing.com/columns/tech-talk/gov-tablets-los-angeles-ipad-apple-schools.html.

Rich, M. (2014, October 16). "Deasy resigns as Los Angeles schools chief after mounting criticism." *New York Times*. Retrieved from: https://www.nytimes.com/2014/10/17/us/lausd-john-deasy-resigns-superintendent-los-angeles.html.

References for Inadvertent Consequences at College—Introduction

Ball, H. (2000). *The Bakke case: Race, education, and affirmative action*. Lawrence, KS: University Press of Kansas.

Chambers, C. R. (2017). *Law and social justice in higher education*. New York: Routledge, 2017.

Stefoff, R. (2006). *The Bakke case: Challenging affirmative action*. New York: Marshall Cavendish Benchmark.

References for Inadvertent Consequences at College—Enthusiasts

Dixon, B. J. (2018, September-October). "Litigating admissions." *Harvard Magazine*. Retrieved from: https://harvardmagazine.com/2018/09/harvard-admissions-lawsuit.

"Top 100 colleges with lowest acceptance rates for 2018." (2018). Educationcorner.com. Retrieved from: https://www.educationcorner.com/colleges-with-lowest-acceptance-rates.html.

References for Inadvertent Consequences at College—Skeptics

Anderson, N. (2018, August 30). "Justice Department criticizes Harvard admissions in case alleging bias against Asian Americans." *Washington Post*. Retrieved from: https://www.washingtonpost.com/education/2018/08/30/justice-dept-criticizes-harvard-affirmative-action-case.

Kennedy, M. (2018, August 30). "Justice Department sides against Harvard in racial discrimination lawsuit." NPR.org. Retrieved from:

https://www.npr.org/2018/08/30/643307030/justice-department-sides-against-harvard-in-racial-discrimination-lawsuit.

Korn, M. (2019, October 1). "Judge rules Harvard's race-conscious admissions policy constitutional." *Wall Street Journal*. Retrieved from: https://www.wsj.com/articles/judge-determines-harvard-s-race-conscious-admissions-policy-is-constitutional-11569958184.

Reilly, K. (2018, October 16). "A lawsuit by Asian-American students against Harvard could end affirmative action as we know it." *Time*. Retrieved from: http://time.com/5425147/harvard-affirmative-action-trial-asian-american-students.

References for Inadvertent Consequences in Public Schools—Introduction

Giordano, G. (2010). *Cockeyed education: A case method primer*. Lanham, MD: Rowman & Littlefield.

Giordano, G. (2011). *Lopsided schools: Case method briefings*. Lanham, MD: Rowman & Littlefield.

Giordano, G. (2012a). *Capping costs: Putting a price tag on school reform*. Lanham, MD: Rowman & Littlefield.

Giordano, G. (2012b). *Teachers go to rehab: Historical and current advice to instructors*. Lanham, MD: Rowman & Littlefield.

Giordano, G. (2015). *Common sense questions about school administration: The answers can provide essential steps to improvement*. Lanham, MD: Rowman & Littlefield.

Giordano, G. (2016). *Common Sense questions about testing: The answers can provide essential steps to improvement*. Lanham, MD: Rowman & Littlefield.

Giordano, G. (2019). *Parents and textbooks: Answers to reveal essential steps to improvement*. Lanham, MD: Rowman & Littlefield.

References for Inadvertent Consequences in Public Schools—Enthusiasts

Gilbertson, A. (2014, August 27). "The LA school iPad scandal: What you need to know." NPR.org. Retrieved from: https://www.npr.org/sections/ed/2014/08/27/343549939/the-l-a-school-ipad-scandal-what-you-need-to-know.

References for Inadvertent Consequences in Public Schools—Skeptics

Blume, H. (2013, October 22). "iPads for L.A. Unified could now cost $770 each, a 14% increase." *Los Angeles Times*. Retrieved from: https://www.latimes.com/local/lanow/la-me-ln-ipads-la-unified-cost-increase-20131022-story.html.

Clough, C. (2015, April 15). "Just in: LAUSD seeking refund for iPads with Pearson software." LAschoolreport.com. Retrieved from: http://

laschoolreport.com/just-in-lausd-seeking-refund-for-ipads-with-pearson-software.

Gilbertson, A. (2014, August 25). "LA schools iPad project: How it started . . . before the bidding began." SCPR.org. Retrieved from: https://www.scpr.org/blogs/education/2014/08/25/17192/how-did-la-schools-decide-on-ipad-software-it-star.

Gilbertson, A. (2015, April 16). "SEC scrutinizing LAUSD's bond-funded iPad program." SCPR.org. Retrieved from: https://www.scpr.org/news/2015/04/16/51070/sec-scrutinizing-lausd-s-bond-funded-ipad-program.

Kohli, S. (2016, April 19). "The cost of L.A. Unified's digital student tracking system rises to $189 million." *Los Angeles Times*. Retrieved from: http://www.latimes.com/local/education/la-me-edu-misis-spending-20160414-snap-story.html.

Lapowsky, S. (2015, April 8). "What school." *Wired*. Retrieved from: https://www.wired.com/2015/05/los-angeles-edtech.

Newcombe, T. (2015, May 13). "A cautionary tale for any government IT project: L.A.'s failed iPad program." Governing.com. Retrieved from: http://www.governing.com/columns/tech-talk/gov-tablets-los-angeles-ipad-apple-schools.html.

REFERENCES FOR CHAPTER 3

References for Beginning of Chapter 3 Quotes

Detroit Federation of Teachers.—*quoted by* Regalado, C., & Lare, R. (2007, January-February). "The Detroit teachers' strike." Solidarity-us.org. Retrieved from: https://www.solidarity-us.org/node/308.

Pavelka, K.—*quoted by* Sedgwick, J. (2018, April 16). "25-Year-old textbooks and holes in the ceiling: Inside America's public schools." *New York Times*. Retrieved from: https://www.nytimes.com/2018/04/16/reader-center/us-public-schools-conditions.html.

Romney, S.—*quoted by* Ravitch, D. (2017, January 18). "Why would anyone listen to Betsy DeVos on the subject of education? It can't be results." *Huffington Post*. Retrieved from: https://www.huffpost.com/entry/betsy-devos-education-results_b_587fb98ae4b0c147f0bc9a81.

Vitti, N.—*quoted by* Clifford, T. (2018, October 10). "Detroit schools to expand computer science curriculum by 2021." *Detroit News*. Retrieved from: https://www.detroitnews.com/story/news/local/detroit-city/2017/09/26/internet-groups-computer-science/106010126/.

References for Road Diets as Inexpensive Cure-Alls—Introduction

Burden, D., & Lagerway, P. (1999). *Road diets: Fixing the big roads.* High Springs, FL: Walkable Communities.

References for Road Diets as Inexpensive Cure-Alls—Enthusiasts

Ewing, R. H., & Brown, S. J. (2017). *U.S. traffic calming manual.* Routledge/Taylor & Francis.
Keatts, A. (2015, September 10). "What are 'road diets,' and why are they controversial?" Kinder.rice. Retrieved from: https://kinder.rice.edu/2015/09/10/what-are-road-diets-and-why-are-they-controversial.
Neuner, M. (2015). *Road diet case studies.* Washington, DC: US Department of Transportation.

References for Road Diets as Inexpensive Cure-Alls—Skeptics

Bauerlein, D. (2018, September 1). "Residents weigh in on 'road diets.'" *Florida Times-Union.* Retrieved from: http://digital.olivesoftware.com/Olive/ODN/FloridaTimesUnion/shared/ShowArticle.aspx?doc=TFTU%2F2018%2F09%2F01&entity=Ar00102&sk=4EB5D64E&mode=text.
Mintz, S., Hahn, E., Nordham, G., & Allday, J. (2017, October 6). "Do drivers who complain about 'road diets' have a better solution to improve cyclists' safety?" *Los Angeles Times.* Retrieved from: https://www.latimes.com/opinion/readersreact/la-ol-le-road-diets-cyclist-safety-playa-del-rey-20171006-story.html.

References for Universal Computer Science Training as an Inexpensive Cure-All—Introduction

Green, E. L. (2017, March 29). "Betsy DeVos calls for more school choice, saying money isn't the answer." *New York Times.* Retrieved from: https://www.nytimes.com/2017/03/29/us/politics/betsy-devos-education-school-choice-voucher.html.
Greenfield, D. (2012, December 12). "Detroit teachers w/$71,000 salaries leave work to protest, while only 7 percent of their students can read." Frontpagemag.com. Retrieved from: http://www.frontpagemag.com/point/169245/detroit-teachers-w71000-salaries-leave-work-daniel-greenfield.
Matheny, K. (2016, May 1). "Detroit teachers union calls for district-wide sick-out Monday." *Detroit Free Press.* Retrieved from: http://www.freep.com/story/news/2016/05/01/detroit-teachers-union-calls-district-wide-sick-out-monday/83798520.
Zernike, K. (2016, December 12). "How Trump's education nominee bent Detroit to her will on charter schools." *New York Times.* Retrieved from: http://www.nytimes.com/2016/12/12/us/politics/betsy-devos-how-

trumps-education-nominee-bent-detroit-to-her-will-on-charter-schools.html.

References for Universal Computer Science Training as an Inexpensive Cure-All—Enthusiasts

    Solomon, L. D. (2018). *Detroit: Three pathways to revitalization*. Oxfordshire, UK: Taylor and Francis.
    Strauss, V. (2018, June 4). "Detroit superintendent: 'This would never ever happen in any white suburban district in this country.'" *Washington Post*. Retrieved from: https://www.washingtonpost.com/news/answer-sheet/wp/2018/06/04/detroit-superintendent-this-would-never-ever-happen-in-any-white-suburban-district-in-this-country /?utm_term=.1932d9938bc5.

References for Universal Computer Science Training as an Inexpensive Cure-All—Skeptics

    Chambers, J. (2018, July 10). "Detroit schools target special ed failures." *Detroit News*. Retrieved from: https://www.detroitnews.com/story/news/local/detroit-city/2018/07/10/detroit-schools-target-ailing-special-ed/739582002.
    "DPS students, parents get 24-7 access to textbooks, assignments, resources." (2011, June 7). CBSlocal.com. Retrieved from: https://detroit.cbslocal.com/2011/06/07/dps-students-parents-get-24-7-access-to-textbooks-assignments-resources.
    Einhorn, E., & Levin, K. (2018, May 17). "A year after Nikolai Vitti arrived in Detroit, a look back at his application shows what's changed." Chalkbeat.org. Retrieved from: https://chalkbeat.org/posts/detroit/2018/05/17/a-year-after-nikolai-vitti-arrived-in-detroit-a-look-back-at-his-application-shows-whats-changed.

REFERENCES FOR CHAPTER 4

References for Beginning of Chapter 4 Quotes

    Calzadilla, J.—*quoted by* Entin, B., & Cohen, D. (2018, August 15). "Miami Springs Senior High student hacked into teachers' computers to change grades." WSVN.com. Retrieved from: https://wsvn.com/news/investigations/miami-springs-senior-high-student-hacked-into-teachers-computers-and-changed-dozens-of-grades.
    Mohney, G. (2014, May 3). "Miami teen arrested for hacking computers to change grades." ABCnews.go.com. Retrieved from: https://abcnews.go.com/US/miami-teen-arrested-hacking-computers-change-grades/story?id=23577368.

Munzenrieder, K. (2014, May 5). "Miami teen hacked school website to change grade, now faces eight." *Miami New Times*. Retrieved from: https://www.miaminewtimes.com/news/miami-teen-hacked-school-website-to-change-grade-now-faces-eight-6551998.

Saad, S.—*quoted by* Hui, T. K. (2017, June 28). "High school hacker who changed grades pays for his actions: Now studies cybertech." *News & Observer*. Retrieved from: https://www.newsobserver.com/news/local/crime/article158637234.html.

References for Predicting the Behavior of a School Leader—Introduction

Miami-Dade Superintendent Alberto Carvalho. (2011, March/April). Educationupdate.com. Retrieved from: http://www.educationupdate.com/archives/2011/MAR/html/spot-miami.html.

Tobin, T. (2018, March 1). "Miami's dramatic day brings it all back: Remember when Alberto Carvalho kept the Pinellas School Board guessing?" *Tampa Bay Times*. Retrieved from: https://www.tampabay.com/blogs/gradebook/2018/03/01/miamis-dramatic-day-brings-it-all-back-remember-when-alberto-carvalho-kept-the-pinellas-school-board-guessing.

References for Predicting the Behavior of a School Leader—Enthusiasts

Harris, E. A. (2018, March 9). "Chancellor's first day in office is set." *New York Times*. Retrieved from: https://www.nytimes.com/2018/03/09/nyregion/carranza-schools-chancellor-start-april-2.html.

Taylor, K. (2018, March 5). "Next to lead New York's schools: An educator with a song on his lips." *New York Times*. Retrieved from: https://www.nytimes.com/2018/03/05/nyregion/richard-carranza-schools-chancellor-new-york-mariachi.html.

References for Predicting the Behavior of a School Leader—Skeptics

Taylor, K., & Goodman, J. D. (2018, March 2). "The match seemed perfect for New York's schools: But there were red flags." *New York Times*. Retrieved from: https://www.nytimes.com/2018/03/02/nyregion/miami-albert-carvalho-new-york-city-schools-chancellor.html.

References for Predicting the Behavior of Computer Science Students—Introduction

Entin, B., & Cohen, D. (2018, August 15). "Miami Springs Senior High student hacked into teachers' computers to change grades." WSVN.com. Retrieved from: https://wsvn.com/news/investigations/miami-springs-senior-high-student-hacked-into-teachers-computers-and-changed-dozens-of-grades/.

Jackson, D. (2014, February 4). "Obama secures money to connect schools to Internet." *USA Today*. Retrieved from: https://www.usatoday.com/story/news/politics/2014/02/04/obama-schools-high-speed-internet-adelphi-maryland/5203225.

Smith, M. (2016, January 30). "Computer science for all." Obamawhitehouse.archives.gov. Retrieved from: https://obamawhitehouse.archives.gov/blog/2016/01/30/computer-science-all.

References for Predicting the Behavior of Computer Science Students—Enthusiasts

Munzenrieder, K. (2014, May 5). "Miami teen hacked school website to change grade, now faces eight." *Miami New Times*. Retrieved from: https://www.miaminewtimes.com/news/miami-teen-hacked-school-website-to-change-grade-now-faces-eight-6551998.

References for Predicting the Behavior of Computer Science Students—Skeptics

Filosa, G. (2018a, September 12). "Keys schools computer system hacked." *Miami Herald*. Retrieved from: https://www.miamiherald.com/latest-news/article218289740.html.

Filosa, G. (2018b, September 13). "Keys public school computers remain down a 5th day after cyberattack." *Miami Herald*. Retrieved from: https://www.miamiherald.com/news/local/community/florida-keys/article218340835.html.

Gurney, K. (2017, June 20). "Are the dangers of cyberattacks targeting school districts being overlooked?" *Government Technology*. Retrieved from: http://www.govtech.com/security/Are-the-Dangers-of-Cyberattacks-Targeting-School-Districts-Being-Overlooked.html.

Hui, T. K. (2017, June 28). "High school hacker who changed grades pays for his actions: Now studies cybertech." *News & Observer*. Retrieved from: https://www.newsobserver.com/news/local/crime/article158637234.html.

Mohney, G. (2014, May 3). "Miami teen arrested for hacking computers to change grades." ABCnews.go.com. Retrieved from: https://abcnews.go.com/US/miami-teen-arrested-hacking-computers-change-grades/story?id=23577368.

REFERENCES FOR CHAPTER 5

References for Beginning of Chapter 5 Quotes

MacAskill, E. (2010, April 20). "US school accused of using laptops to spy on pupils." *Guardian*. Retrieved from: https://www.theguardian.com/world/2010/apr/20/us-school-accused-laptops-spying.

McGinley, C.—*quoted by* Nasaw, D. (2010, February 19). "US school district spied on students through webcams, court told." *Guardian*. Retrieved from: https://www.theguardian.com/world/2010/feb/19/schools-spied-on-students-webcams.

Nasaw, D. (2010, February 19). "US school district spied on students through webcams, court told." *Guardian*. Retrieved from: https://www.theguardian.com/world/2010/feb/19/schools-spied-on-students-webcams.

Robbins, H.—*quoted in* "$610K settlement in school webcam spy case." (October 21, 2010). CBSnews.com. Retrieved from: https://www.cbsnews.com/news/610k-settlement-in-school-webcam-spy-case.

References for Deceptive Diplomas—Introduction

Lancaster, T. (2017, January 31). "Everything you need to know about fake degrees and the 'universities' awarding them." Theconversation.com. Retrieved from: http://theconversation.com/everything-you-need-to-know-about-fake-degrees-and-the-universities-awarding-them-71132.

Walsh, D. (2015, May 17). "Fake diplomas, real cash: Pakistani company Axact reaps millions." *New York Times*. Retrieved from: http://www.nytimes.com/2015/05/18/world/asia/fake-diplomas-real-cash-pakistani-company-axact-reaps-millions-columbiana-barkley.html.

References for Deceptive Diplomas —Enthusiasts

Hensley-Clancy, M. (2016, April 15). "Students at fake university say they are 'victims' of government sting." *BuzzFeed News*. Retrieved from: https://www.buzzfeednews.com/article/mollyhensleyclancy/students-at-fake-university-say-theyre-victims-of-government.

Imtiaz, S., & Walsh, D. (2015, May 19). "Pakistani investigators raid offices of Axact, fake diploma company." *New York Times*. Retrieved from: http://www.nytimes.com/2015/05/20/world/asia/pakistani-investigators-raid-offices-of-axact-fake-diploma-company.html.

Mackey, R. (2015, May 1). "Axact, fake diploma company, threatens Pakistani bloggers who laugh at its expense." *New York Times*. Retrieved from: https://www.nytimes.com/2015/05/19/world/asia/axact-fake-diploma-company-threatens-pakistani-bloggers-who-laugh-at-its-expense.html.

Waddell, K. (2015, July 15). "How a federal employee with fake diplomas worked at the Department of the Interior for five years." *Atlantic*. Retrieved from: https://www.theatlantic.com/politics/archive/2015/07/how-a-federal-employee-with-fake-diplomas-worked-at-the-department-of-the-interior-for-five-years/458424.

References for Deceptive Diplomas —Skeptics

Farzan, A. F. (2019, January 31). "ICE set up a fake university: Hundreds enrolled, not realizing it was a sting operation." *Washington Post*. Retrieved from: https://www.washingtonpost.com/nation/2019/01/31/ice-set-up-fake-university-hundreds-enrolled-not-realizing-it-was-sting-operation/?noredirect=on&utm_term=.aadc80b92215.

Imtiaz, S. (2015, May 23). "Pakistani journalists resign to cut ties to Axact, a fake diploma company." *New York Times*. Retrieved from: http://www.nytimes.com/2015/05/24/world/asia/pakistan-says-it-has-evidence-against-axact-a-fake-diploma-company.html.

Walsh, D. (2015, May 22). "Pakistan widens inquiry into fake diplomas." *New York Times*. Retrieved from: http://www.nytimes.com/2015/05/23/world/asia/pakistan-widens-inquiry-into-fake-diplomas.html.

References for Deceptive Computers—Introduction

"Chair Joyce Wilkerson and Dr. Chris McGinley announce their resignations as SRC plans for transition." (2018, March 29). Phila.gov. Retrieved from: https://www.philasd.org/blog/2018/03/29/chair-joyce-wilkerson-and-dr-chris-mcginley-announce-their-resignations-as-src-plans-for-transition.

Fisk, S. (2018, June 27). "Meet your new Board of Education member: Chris McGinley." Phila.gov. Retrieved from: https://www.phila.gov/2018-06-27-meet-your-new-board-of-education-member-chris-mcginley.

References for Deceptive Computers —Enthusiasts

"$610K settlement in school webcam spy case." (2010, October 21). CBSnews.com. Retrieved from: https://www.cbsnews.com/news/610k-settlement-in-school-webcam-spy-case.

Hill, K. (2016, March 31). "'Dozens' of student suicides prevented by schools spying on everything they do on their computers." Splinternews.com. Retrieved from: https://splinternews.com/dozens-of-student-suicides-prevented-by-schools-spying-1793855919.

References for Deceptive Computers — Skeptics

Betancur, M. (2017, June 15). "In Rhode Island, some schools think they have the right to spy on students with school laptops." *American Civil Liberties Union*. Retrieved from: https://www.aclu.org/blog/privacy-technology/internet-privacy/rhode-island-some-schools-think-they-have-right-spy.

Gebhart, G. (2017, April 13). "Spying on students: School-issued devices and student privacy." Electronic Frontier Foundation. Retrieved from: https://www.eff.org/wp/school-issued-devices-and-student-privacy.

Jones, A. (2010, October 21). "Alex Jones on school webcam spying scandal in Philadelphia." Youtube.com. Retrieved from: https://www.youtube.com/watch?v=lp9xWeT98zQ&feature=youtu.be.

Keizer, G. (2010, February 18). "Pennsylvania schools spying on students using laptop webcams, claims lawsuit." *Computerworld*. Retrieved from: https://www.computerworld.com/article/2521075/windows-pcs/pennsylvania-schools-spying-on-students-using-laptop-webcams--claims-lawsuit.html.

Kravets, D. (2010, April 16). "School district allegedly snapped thousands of student webcam spy pics." *Wired*. Retrieved from: https://www.wired.com/2010/04/webcamscanda.

Leyden, J. (2010, August 19). "PA school district avoids charges over webcam spy scandal." *The Register*. Retrieved from: https://www.theregister.co.uk/2010/08/19/school_webcam_spying_no_crime.

REFERENCES FOR CHAPTER 6

References for Beginning of Chapter 6 Quotes

DeSantis, R. — *quoted by* Kam, D. (2019, February 14). "DeSantis calls for school safety probe." *Florida Times-Union*. Retrieved from: http://digital.olivesoftware.com/olive/odn/floridatimesunion/shared/showarticle.aspx?doc=tftu%2f2019%2f02%2f14&entity=ar00202&sk=dc5759ca&mode=text.

Ferguson, T. — *quoted by* Reeves, M., & Solochek, J. S. (2018, July 27). "Florida's sobering new focus on school security creates a challenge: How to protect and not stoke fear." *Tampa Bay Times*. Retrieved from: https://www.tampabay.com/news/education/k12/Florida-s-sobering-new-focus-on-school-security-creates-a-challenge-How-to-protect-and-not-stoke-fear-_170124316.

McDonald, K. (2019, January 8). "School security is now a $3 billion dollar [sic] annual industry." Foundation for Economic Education. Retrieved from: https://fee.org/articles/school-security-is-now-a-3-billion-dollar-annual-industry-is-there-a-better-way-to-protect-kids/.

Stafford, C.—*quoted by* Kennedy, J. (2018, March 7). "House GOP rejects Dems' efforts to change gun bill." *Florida Times-Union*. Retrieved from: http://digital.olivesoftware.com/Olive/ODN/FloridaTimesUnion/shared/ShowArticle.aspx?doc=TFTU%2F2018%2F03%2F07&entity=Ar00102&sk=05C938D4&mode=text.

References for Expanding Daylight Savings Time—Introduction

Downing, M. (2006). *Spring forward: The annual madness of daylight saving*. Washington, DC: Shoemaker & Hoard.

Victor, D. (2016, March 11). "Daylight Saving Time: Why does it exist?" *New York Times*. Retrieved from: http://www.nytimes.com/2016/03/12/us/daylight-saving-time-farmers.html.

References for Expanding Daylight Savings Time —Enthusiasts

Diaz, A. (2018, March 7). "Florida lawmakers vote to stay in Daylight Saving Time all year long." CNN.com. Retrieved from: https://www.cnn.com/2018/03/07/us/florida-year-round-daylight-saving-time-trnd/index.html.

References for Expanding Daylight Savings Time—Skeptics

Murse, T. (2018, March 3). "Who enforces Daylight Saving Time?" Thoughtco.com. Retrieved from: https://www.thoughtco.com/who-enforces-daylight-saving-time-3321062.

References for Expanding School Safety Tech—Introduction

Amos, D. S. (2018, November 14). "District wants 2 metal detectors per high school." *Florida Times-Union*. Retrieved from: http://digital.olivesoftware.com/Olive/ODN/FloridaTimesUnion/shared/ShowArticle.aspx?doc=TFTU%2F2018%2F11%2F14&entity=Ar00103&sk=B151F817&mode=text.

May, D. C. (2014). *School safety in the United States: A reasoned look at the rhetoric*. Durham, NC: Carolina Academic Press.

Timm, P. (2015). *School security: How to build and strengthen a school safety program*. Waltham, MA: Butterworth-Heinemann.

Ujifusa, A. (2018, February 28). "Trump pushes to 'harden' schools against mass shooters in meeting with lawmakers." *Education Week*. Retrieved from: http://blogs.edweek.org/edweek/campaign-k-12/2018/02/trump_pushes_to_harden_schools_mass_shooters_lawmakers.html.

References for Expanding School Safety Tech—Enthusiasts

Bloch, E. (2019, May 17). "Duval renews student safety partnership." *Florida Times Union*. Retrieved from: http://digital.olivesoftware.com/Olive/ODN/FloridaTimesUnion/shared/ShowArticle.aspx?doc=TFTU%2F2019%2F05%2F17&entity=Ar00902&sk=892C0540&mode=text.

Blazonis, S. (2018, September 27). "Upgraded door locks, cameras among security recommendations for Pasco schools." Baynews9.com. Retrieved from: https://www.baynews9.com/fl/tampa/news/2018/09/27/pasco-schools-get-security-recommendations.

Davis, J. (2018, October 3). "Assessments lead to security upgrades at Tampa Bay schools." Campuslifesecurity.com. Retrieved from: https://campuslifesecurity.com/articles/2018/10/03/assessments-lead-to-security-upgrades-at-tampa-bay-schools.aspx.

Dazio, S. (2019, May 17). "Turning to tech for security." *Florida Times Union*. Retrieved from: http://digital.olivesoftware.com/Olive/ODN/FloridaTimesUnion/shared/ShowArticle.aspx?doc=TFTU%2F2019%2F05%2F17&entity=Ar01200&sk=8AABD5F1&mode=text.

Eakins, J. (2018). "Protecting HCPS students and personnel." Sdhc.k12.fl.us. Retrieved from: https://www.sdhc.k12.fl.us/departments/9/security/about.

Rock, A. (2018, May 14). "Florida schools struggle to fund SROs, adjust safety plans." Campussafetymagazine.com. Retrieved from: https://www.campussafetymagazine.com/safety/florida-schools-sro.

"School districts around Tampa Bay release statements on what they're doing for school security. (2018, August 8). *Tampa Bay Times*. Retrieved from: https://www.wtsp.com/article/entertainment/television/studio10/education/school-districts-around-tampa-bay-release-statements-on-what-theyre-doing-for-school-security/67-574120753.

References for Expanding School Safety Tech—Skeptics

Kennedy, J. (2018, March 7). "House GOP rejects Dems' efforts to change gun bill." *Florida Times-Union*. Retrieved from: http://digital.olivesoftware.com/Olive/ODN/FloridaTimesUnion/shared/ShowArticle.aspx?doc=TFTU%2F2018%2F03%2F07&entity=Ar00102&sk=05C938D4&mode=text.

Kennedy, J. (2019, April 5). "Students protest Legislature's intention to arm teachers." *Florida Times-Union*. Retrieved from: http://digital.olivesoftware.com/Olive/ODN/FloridaTimesUnion/shared/ShowArticle.aspx?doc=TFTU%2F2019%2F04%2F05&entity=Ar01104&sk=56449173&mode=text.

Mencimer, S. (2018, February 22). "The NRA's plan to 'harden' schools is terrifying." *Mother Jones*. Retrieved from:https://www.motherjones.com/politics/2018/02/the-nras-plan-to-harden-schools-is-terrifying/.

Solochek, J. (2018, February 23). "Gov. Rick Scott opposes arming Florida school teachers." *Tampa Bay Times*. Retrieved from: https://www.tampabay.com/blogs/gradebook/2018/02/23/gov-rick-scott-opposes-arming-florida-school-teachers/.

Warnick, B., B. A. Johnson, & S. Rocha. (2018, February 15). "Can security measures really stop school shootings?" *Scientific American*. Retrieved from: https://www.scientificamerican.com/article/can-security-measures-really-stop-school-shootings.

REFERENCES FOR CHAPTER 7

References for Beginning of Chapter 7 Quotes

Batchelor, M. (2018, March 1). "Judge bans 16-year-old from violent video games over school shooting threat." Gamesindustry.biz. Retrieved from: https://www.gamesindustry.biz/articles/2018-03-01-judge-bans-16-year-old-from-violent-video-games-over-school-shooting-threat.

Gold, P.—*quoted by* Cohen, H. (2018, March 1). "The Parkland shooting inspires school leader to campaign against violent video games." *Miami Herald*. Retrieved from: https://www.miamiherald.com/news/local/education/article202674159.html.

Hull, J.—*quoted by* Snider, M. (2018, October 2). "Study confirms link between violent video games and physical aggression." *USA Today*. Retrieved from: https://www.usatoday.com/story/tech/news/2018/10/01/violent-video-games-tie-physical-aggression-confirmed-study/1486188002.

Unidentified Blogger—*quoted in* Dookey. (2018, March 2). "Judge bans sophomore from violent video games after threat." Hardforum.com. Retrieved from: https://hardforum.com/threads/judge-bans-sophomore-from-violent-video-games-after-threat.1955551.

References for Post Office–Linked Violence—Introduction

Baxter V. K. (1994). "Workplace violence in the U.S. Post Office." In: Baxter, V. K. (Ed.). *Labor and Politics in the U.S. Postal Service. (Springer Studies in Work and Industry)*. (pp. 187–199). Boston: Springer.

Davids, J. (2011, November 14). "20 Years later: A look back at Royal Oak Post Office shootings." Patch.com. Retrieved from: https://patch.com/michigan/royaloak/a-look-back-at-the-royal-oak-postal-shootings.

References for Post Office–Linked Violence—Enthusiasts

Committee on Post Office and Civil Service. (1987). *Events of August 20, 1986, in Edmond, OK: Joint hearing before the Subcommittee on Postal Operations and Services and the Subcommittee on Postal Personnel and Modernization of the Committee on Post Office and Civil Service, House of Representatives, One hundredth Congress, first session, March 18, 1987*. Washington, DC: US Government Printing Office.

Hanley, R. (1991, October 1). "4 slain in 2 New Jersey attacks and former postal clerk is held." *New York Times*. Retrieved from: https://www.nytimes.com/1991/10/11/nyregion/4-slain-in-2-new-jersey-attacks-and-former-postal-clerk-is-held.html.

Kilborn, P. T. (1993, May 17). "Inside post offices, the mail is only part of the pressure." *New York Times*. Retrieved from: https://www.nytimes.com/1993/05/17/us/inside-post-offices-the-mail-is-only-part-of-the-pressure.html.

Levin, D. P. (1991, November 15). "Ex-postal worker kills 3 and wounds 6 in Michigan." *New York Times*. Retrieved from: https://www.nytimes.com/1991/11/15/us/ex-postal-worker-kills-3-and-wounds-6-in-michigan.html.

Lisi, B. (2016, October 11). "A look at some of the worst postal worker-related incidents on the 25th anniversary of the Ridgewood, NJ shooting." *New York Daily News*. Retrieved from: https://www.nydailynews.com/news/crime/worst-postal-worker-related-incidents-article-1.2826721.

Mydans, S. (1993, May 7). "2 Are killed in post office shootings in 2 states." *New York Times*. Retrieved from: https://www.nytimes.com/1993/05/07/us/2-are-killed-in-post-office-shootings-in-2-states.html.

New York Times Editorial Board. (1993, May 19). "Violence in the post office." *New York Times*. Retrieved from: https://www.nytimes.com/1993/05/19/opinion/violence-in-the-post-office.html.

US Postal Service. (2009). *Achieving a violence-free workplace together* (Publication #45). Author. Retrieved from: https://www.nalc.org/workplace-issues/resources/manuals/other/PUB_45.pdf.

US Postal Service. (2019). *Violence prevention and crisis management*. Author. Retrieved from: https://about.usps.com/strategic-planning/cs09/CSPO_09_099.htm.

References for Post Office–Linked Violence—Skeptics

"Healthcare workers have highest rate of workplace violence." (2019). American Medical Resource Institute. Retrieved from: https://www.aclsonline.us/articles/healthcare-workers-have-highest-rate-of-workplace-violences.

Kelloway, E. K., Barling, J., & Hurrell, J. J. (Eds.). (2013). *Handbook of workplace violence*. Thousand Oaks, CA: Sage.

Kerr, K. (2016). *Workplace violence: Planning for prevention and response.* Oxford: Elsevier/Butterworth-Heinemann.

Neuman, J. H. (1998, June). "Workplace violence and workplace aggression: Evidence concerning specific forms, potential causes, and preferred targets." *Journal of Management.* Retrieved from: https://www.researchgate.net/profile/Joel_Neuman/publication/254121227_Workplace_Violence_and_Workplace_Aggression_Evidence_Concerning_Specific_Forms_Potential_Causes_and_Preferred_Targets/links/54b877760cf28faced621301/Workplace-Violence-and-Workplace-Aggression-Evidence-Concerning-Specific-Forms-Potential-Causes-and-Preferred-Targets.pdf.

Paludi, M. A., Nydegger, R. V., & Paludi, C. A. (2007). *Understanding workplace violence: A guide for managers and employees.* Westport, CT: Praeger.

US Occupational Safety and Health Administration. (2002, February 14). *Workplace violence.* US Department of Labor. Retrieved from: https://www.osha.gov/archive/oshinfo/priorities/violence.html.

References for Video Game–Linked School Violence—Introduction

Cohen, H. (2018, March 1). "The Parkland shooting inspires school leader to campaign against violent video games." *Miami Herald.* Retrieved from: https://www.miamiherald.com/news/local/education/article202674159.html.

Entertainment Software Rating Board. (2018). "How does the ratings process work?" ESRB.org. Retrieved from: http://www.esrb.org/ratings/ratings_guide.aspx.

Gonchar, M. (2016, September 27). "Are the web filters at your school too restrictive?" *New York Times.* Retrieved from: https://www.nytimes.com/2016/09/27/learning/are-the-web-filters-at-your-school-too-restrictive.html.

Hill, K. (2016, March 31). "'Dozens' of student suicides prevented by schools spying on everything they do on their computers." Splinternews.com. Retrieved from: https://splinternews.com/dozens-of-student-suicides-prevented-by-schools-spying-1793855919.

Lebedev, A. (2017, March 3). "Should video games be banned in school?" Quora.com. Retrieved from: https://www.quora.com/Should-video-games-be-banned-in-school.

Microsoft Corporation. (2018). "Block inappropriate apps, games, and media on Windows 10 and Xbox One." Microsoft.com. Retrieved from: https://support.microsoft.com/en-us/help/4026341/microsoft-account-block-inappropriate-apps-games-media.

Mosyle Corporation. (2018). "MDM features that can avoid students from playing games during class." Mosyle.com. Retrieved from: https://

manager.mosyle.com/itinsights/mdm-features-that-can-avoid-students-from-playing-games-during-class.

New Beginnings Drug and Alcohol Rehabilitation Center. (2018). *Understanding and preventing video game addiction.* Author. Retrieved from: https://www.newbeginningsdrugrehab.org/video-game-addiction.

Schwartz, S. (2018, May 3). "Educators battle 'Fortnite' for students' attention." *Education Week.* Retrieved from: https://www.edweek.org/ew/articles/2018/05/03/educators-battle-fortnite-for-students-attention.html.

Snider, M. (2018, October 2). "Study confirms link between violent video games and physical aggression." *USA Today.* Retrieved from: https://www.usatoday.com/story/tech/news/2018/10/01/violent-video-games-tie-physical-aggression-confirmed-study/1486188002.

Wagner, S. (2018). "Internet filtering software for schools: Pros and cons." Hertzfurniture.com. Retrieved from: https://www.hertzfurniture.com/buying-guide/education-resources/school-internet-filters.html.

References for Video Game–Linked School Violence — Enthusiasts

Batchelor, M. (2018, March 1). "Judge bans 16-year-old from violent video games over school shooting threat." Gamesindustry.biz. Retrieved from: https://www.gamesindustry.biz/articles/2018-03-01-judge-bans-16-year-old-from-violent-video-games-over-school-shooting-threat.

Berson, S. (2018, March 1). "No more violent video games, judge tells teen accused of making threat against school." *Miami Herald.* Retrieved from: https://www.miamiherald.com/article202928884.html.

Campbell, C. (2018, February 28). "Chicago high school sophomore ordered to stay away from violent games." Polygon.com. Retrieved from: https://www.polygon.com/2018/2/28/17065226/school-shooting-threat-violent-video-game-ban.

Khan, I. (2018, March 1). "Judge bans teen from violent video games after shooting threat." Gameinformer.com. Retrieved from: https://www.gameinformer.com/b/news/archive/2018/03/01/judge-bans-teen-from-violent-video-games-after-shooting-threat.aspx.

Twenge, J. M. (2018). *iGen: Why today's super-connected kids are growing up less rebellious, more tolerant, less happy.* New York: Atria International.

References for Video Game–Linked School Violence — Skeptics

Dookey. (2018, March 2). "Judge bans sophomore from violent video games after threat." Hardforum.com. Retrieved from: https://hardforum.com/threads/judge-bans-sophomore-from-violent-video-games-after-threat.1955551.

Fogel, S. (2018, April 19). "High school esports competitions to begin in U.S. this year." *Variety.* Retrieved from: https://variety.com/2018/gaming/news/high-school-esports-1202758438.

Hennick, C. (2019, January 11). "Esports programs start to pop up in K–12 schools." Edtechmagazine.com. Retrieved from: https://edtechmagazine.com/k12/article/2019/01/esports-programs-start-pop-k-12-schools.

Jargon, J. (2019, April 2). "Why videogames trigger the nightly meltdown—and how to help your child cope." *Wall Street Journal*. Retrieved from: https://www.wsj.com/articles/why-videogames-trigger-the-nightly-meltdownand-how-to-help-your-child-cope-11554206405.

McGrath, B. S. (2019, September 20). "High school gamers are scoring college scholarships: But can esports make varsity?" NBCnews.com. Retrieved from: https://www.nbcnews.com/tech/video-games/high-school-gamers-are-scoring-college-scholarships-can-esports-make-n1056671.

Melia, M. (2019, January 20). "Why US classrooms are starting to resemble arcades." *Florida Times-Union*. Retrieved from: http://digital.olivesoftware.com/Olive/ODN/FloridaTimesUnion/shared/ShowArticle.aspx?doc=TFTU%2F2019%2F01%2F20&entity=Ar04902&sk=5B2058EB&mode=text.

Paul, A. M. (2014, July 2). "Why schools' efforts to block the Internet are so laughably lame." *Hechinger Report*. Retrieved from: https://hechingerreport.org/schools-efforts-block-internet-laughably-lame.

Shapiro, J. (2018). *The new childhood: Raising kids to thrive in a connected world*. New York: Little, Brown/Spark.

Starr, L. (2007, April 30). "Filtering software: The educators speak out." *Education World*. Retrieved from: https://www.educationworld.com/a_tech/tech155.shtml.

Wagner, S. (2018). "Internet filtering software for schools: Pros and cons." Hertzfurniture.com. Retrieved from: https://www.hertzfurniture.com/buying-guide/education-resources/school-internet-filters.html.

Wright, W., & Baker, C. (2012, August 14). "Interview: Will Wright wants to make a game out of life itself." *Wired*. Retrieved from: https://www.wired.co.uk/article/the-creator.

REFERENCES FOR CHAPTER 8

References for Beginning of Chapter 8 Quotes

Jobs, S.—*quoted in* Weller, C. (2017, November 7). "An MIT psychologist explains why so many tech moguls send their kids to anti-tech schools." Businessinsider.com. Retrieved from: https://www.businessinsider.com/sherry-turkle-why-tech-moguls-send-their-kids-to-anti-tech-schools-2017-11.

Nadella, S. (2017, June 13). "Learn more about Microsoft in education [video]." *Microsoft Reporter*. Retrieved from: http://event.microsoft.com/MayEvent.

Turkle, S. — *quoted in* Weller, C. (2017, November 7). "An MIT psychologist explains why so many tech moguls send their kids to anti-tech schools." Businessinsider.com. Retrieved from: https://www.businessinsider.com/sherry-turkle-why-tech-moguls-send-their-kids-to-anti-tech-schools-2017-11.

Unidentified Parent. — *quoted in* Morris, B., & Hobbs, T. D. (2019, September 3). "Schools pushed for tech in every classroom. Now parents are pushing back." *Wall Street Journal*. Retrieved from: https://www.wsj.com/articles/in-a-school-district-where-technology-rules-grades-fall-parents-ask-why-11567523719.

References for Expanding . . . and Reducing . . . Healthy Menu Items — Introduction

"Brand value of the 10 most valuable fast food brands worldwide in 2018 (in million U.S. dollars)." (2019). Statista.com. Retrieved from: https://www.statista.com/statistics/273057/value-of-the-most-valuable-fast-food-brands-worldwide.

"Burger King (BKW) shows strength on sales initiatives." (2014, November 26). Nasdaq.com. Retrieved from: https://www.nasdaq.com/articles/burger-king-bkw-shows-strength-on-sales-initiatives-analyst-blog-2014-11-26.

Jones, E. (2018, July 24). "9 of the healthiest things you can order in McDonald's." *Cosmopolitan*. Retrieved from: https://www.cosmopolitan.com/uk/body/health/news/a46171/healthiest-thing-you-order-mcdonalds.

Malacoff, J. (2018, February 22). "The healthiest things you can order from the McDonald's menu, according to nutritionists." Shape.com. Retrieved from: https://www.shape.com/healthy-eating/meal-ideas/healthiest-orders-mcdonalds-menu.

"Market share of leading brands in the United States fast food industry in 2015." (2019). Statista.com. Retrieved from: https://www.statista.com/statistics/196611/market-share-of-fast-food-restaurant-corporations-in-the-us/.

Nelson, B. (2018, January 11). "The 5 healthiest things to order at McDonald's, according to a nutritionist." Businessinsider.com. Retrieved from: https://www.businessinsider.com/healthiest-things-to-order-at-mcdonalds-2018-1.

References for Expanding . . . and Reducing . . . Healthy Menu Items — Enthusiasts

BoscoW52. (2016, May 4). "About Burger King." Tripadvisor.com. Retrieved from: https://www.tripadvisor.com/ShowUserReviews-g52612-d4955717-r370212309-Burger_King-Etters_Pennsylvania.html#.

"Did Burger King have grilled hot dogs?" (2020, November 22). Burgerbeast.com. Retrieved from: https://burgerbeast.com/burger-king-hot-dog/.

Jargon, J. (2016, February 10). "Burger King to start selling hot dogs." *Wall Street Journal*. Retrieved from: http://www.wsj.com/articles/burger-king-to-start-selling-hot-dogs-1455123632.

Whitten, S. (2016, February 12). "Burger King's newest menu item: Grilled dogs." CNBC.com. Retrieved from: https://www.cnbc.com/2016/02/10/burger-kings-newest-menu-item-grilled-dogs.html?&qsearchterm=Burger King's newest menu item: Grilled dogs.

References for Expanding . . . and Reducing . . . Healthy Menu Items—Skeptics

"Burger King financial problems." (2012, May 7). Wealthartisan.com. Retrieved from: https://wealthartisan.com/burger-king-problems.

Cuozzo, S. (2016, March 2). "Burger King's hot dogs are a disgusting disgrace." *New York Post*. Retrieved from: https://nypost.com/2016/03/02/burger-kings-hot-dogs-are-a-disgusting-disgrace/.

Haddon, H., & Monga, V. (2019, May 15). "Burger King parent defends strategy as growth cools." *Wall Street Journal*. Retrieved from: https://www.wsj.com/articles/burger-king-parent-defends-strategy-as-growth-cools-11557912600.

Hill, J. (2016, February 23). "Burger King hot dog review: I might be dead by the weekend." Fansided.com. Retrieved from: https://fansided.com/2016/02/23/burger-king-hot-dogs-review.

Patton, L., & Giammona, C. (2017, April 26). "Burger King's owner tumbles as chain loses ground to McDonald's." *Bloomberg News*. Retrieved from: https://www.bloomberg.com/news/articles/2017-04-26/burger-king-sales-slip-in-sign-it-s-losing-ground-in-burger-wars.

References for Expanding . . . and Reducing . . . School Tech—Introduction

"About Silicon Valley High School." (2019). SVHS.co. Retrieved from: https://svhs.co/about.

Bacon, D. (2014, October 2). "Silicon Valley breeding nationwide schools-for-profit scheme." *Peoples World*. Retrieved from: https://www.peoplesworld.org/article/silicon-valley-breeding-nationwide-schools-for-profit-scheme/.

Kennedy Middle School. (2019). "Cupertino Union School District." Retrieved from: https://www.cusdk8.org/domain/1111.

Richtel, M. (2011, October 22). "A Silicon Valley school that doesn't compute." *New York Times*. Retrieved from: https://www.nytimes.com/2011/10/23/technology/at-waldorf-school-in-silicon-valley-technology-can-wait.html.

"Silicon Valley High School." (2019). Greatschools.org. Retrieved from: https://www.greatschools.org/california/scotts-valley/31595-Silicon-Valley-High-School.

"Top-rated schools in Silicon Valley." (2019). Davidandsunny.com. Retrieved from: http://davidandsunny.com/top-rated-schools-silicon-valley.

Weller, C. (2017, November 7). "An MIT psychologist explains why so many tech moguls send their kids to anti-tech schools." Businessinsider.com. Retrieved from: https://www.businessinsider.com/sherry-turkle-why-tech-moguls-send-their-kids-to-anti-tech-schools-2017-11.

References for Expanding . . . and Reducing . . . School Tech—Enthusiasts

Homayoun, A. (2018, December 27). "How much screen time?" *Washington Post*. Retrieved from: https://www.washingtonpost.com/lifestyle/2018/12/27/how-much-screentime-debate-all-parents-are-just-trying-figure-it-out/?utm_term=.288d61902159.

Nathani, K. (2018, August 30). "The techpreneurs of Silicon Valley are keeping their families away from technology—Should you too?" Entrepreneur.com. Retrieved from: https://www.entrepreneur.com/article/319288.

Rideout, V. (2018, September 10). "Common Sense research reveals everything you need to know about teens' use of social media in 2018." Commonsensemedia.org. Retrieved from: https://www.commonsensemedia.org/about-us/news/press-releases/common-sense-research-reveals-everything-you-need-to-know-about-teens.

Smith, R. (2018, July 31). "France bans smartphones from schools." CNN. Retrieved from: https://www.cnn.com/2018/07/31/europe/france-smartphones-school-ban-intl/index.html.

Wooster, M. M. (2018, May 25). "The spectacular failure of one laptop per child." Capitalresearch.org. Retrieved from: https://capitalresearch.org/article/the-spectacular-failure-of-one-laptop-per-child.

References for Expanding . . . and Reducing . . . School Tech—Skeptics

Fairlie, R. W., & Robinson, J. (2013, May). "Experimental evidence on the effects of home computers on academic achievement among schoolchildren." *American Economic Journal: Applied Economics*, 5, 211–240. Retrieved from: https://www.nber.org/papers/w19060.

Richtel, M. (2011, October 22). "A Silicon Valley school that doesn't compute." *New York Times*. Retrieved from: https://www.nytimes.com/2011/10/23/technology/at-waldorf-school-in-silicon-valley-technology-can-wait.html.

REFERENCES FOR CHAPTER 9

References for Beginning of Chapter 9 Quotes

Lowry, B.—*quoted by* Wilson, C., & Murphy, J. (2019, April 2). "State computer testing vendor comes under fire after second year of exam glitches." Lohud.com. Retrieved from: https://www.lohud.com/story/news/education/2019/04/02/ny-online-testing-vendor-questar-faces-criticism-glitches/3346172002.

New York State Department of Education. (2019). *Computer-based testing*. Author. Retrieved from: http://www.nysed.gov/edtech/computer-based-testing-cbt.

New York State United Teachers. (2019, April 3). "New York State must stop computer-based testing immediately." Author. Retrieved from: https://www.nysut.org/news/2019/april/new-york-state-must-stop-computer-based-testing-immediately.

Nichols, J., & Stone, A. (2018, January 19). "NYC parents boycott standardized tests." Teachhub.com. Retrieved from: http://www.teachhub.com/nyc-parents-boycott-standardized-tests.

References for Problematic Bar Exams—Introduction

Craven, J. (2019, January 29). "Bar exam pass rate by state." Lawschooli.com. Retrieved from: https://lawschooli.com/bar-exam-pass-rate-by-state.

Miller, C. (2018, December 29). "2018 California's bar exam: How schools fared and what questions a new analysis didn't answer." Law.com. Retrieved from: https://www.law.com/therecorder/2018/12/29/californias-bar-exam-how-schools-fared-and-what-questions-a-new-analysis-didnt-answer.

Olson, E. (2015, April 26). "Burdened with debt, law school graduates struggle in job market." *New York Times*. Retrieved from: https://www.nytimes.com/2015/04/27/business/dealbook/burdened-with-debt-law-school-graduates-struggle-in-job-market.html.

State Bar of California. (2019). "California bar examination statistics." Author. Retrieved from: https://www.calbar.ca.gov/Admissions/Law-School-Regulation/Exam-Statistics.

References for Problematic Bar Exams—Enthusiasts

Randazzo, S. (2019, January 13). "New test for law schools: Do enough graduates pass the bar?" *Wall Street Journal*. Retrieved from: https://www.wsj.com/articles/new-test-for-law-schools-do-enough-graduates-pass-the-bar-11547391600.

Sloan, K. (2019, January 22). "ABA to reconsider proposal to tighten bar exam pass standards." Law.com. Retrieved from: https://www.law.com/2019/01/22/aba-reconsiders-proposal-to-tighten-bar-exam-pass-standards/?slreturn=20190512154919.

Zaretsky, S. (2019, May 20). "With second-worst pass rate in more than 30 years, almost everyone fails California bar exam." Abovethelaw.com. Retrieved from: https://abovethelaw.com/2019/05/with-second-worst-pass-rate-in-more-than-30-years-almost-everyone-fails-california-bar-exam.

References for Problematic Bar Exams—Skeptics

Caron, P. (2019, January 29). "ABA House of Delegates again rejects 75% bar passage within 2 years accreditation standard, 79% to 21%; Final decision rests with Council." TaxProf Blog. Retrieved from: https://taxprof.typepad.com/taxprof_blog/2019/01/aba-house-of-delegates-again-rejects-75-bar-passage-within-2-years-accreditation-standard-79-to-21-f.html.

References for Problematic School Exams—Introduction

Giordano, G. (2000). *Twentieth-century reading education: Understanding practices of today in terms of patterns of the past.* London, UK: Elsevier/JAI Press.

Giordano, G. (2003). *Twentieth-century textbook wars: A history of advocacy and opposition.* New York: Peter Lang.

Giordano, G. (2005). *How testing came to dominate American schools: The history of educational assessment.* New York: Peter Lang.

Giordano, G. (2009). *Solving education problems effectively: A guide to using the case method.* Lanham, MD: Rowman & Littlefield.

Giordano, G. (2010). *Cockeyed education: A case method primer.* Lanham, MD: Rowman & Littlefield.

Giordano, G. (2011). *Lopsided school: Case method briefings.* Lanham, MD: Rowman & Littlefield.

Giordano, G. (2012a). *Capping costs: Putting a price tag on school reform.* Lanham, MD: Rowman & Littlefield.

Giordano, G. (2012b). *Teachers go to rehab: Historical and current advice to instructors.* Lanham, MD: Rowman & Littlefield.

Giordano, G. (2014). *Commonsense questions about instruction: The answers can provide essential steps to improvement.* Lanham, MD: Rowman & Littlefield.

Giordano, G. (2015). *Common sense questions about school administration: The answers can provide essential steps to improvement.* Lanham, MD: Rowman & Littlefield.

Giordano, G. (2016). *Common sense questions about testing: The answers can provide essential steps to improvement.* Lanham, MD: Rowman & Littlefield.

Giordano, G. (2017). *Common sense questions about learners: Answers to reveal essential steps to improvement.* Lanham, MD: Rowman & Littlefield.

References for Problematic School Exams—Enthusiasts

Arnold, C. (2019, January 14). "Privacy in schools: How New York plans to protect your child's personal information." *Democrat and Chronicle.* Retrieved from: https://www.democratandchronicle.com/story/news/politics/albany/2019/01/14/privacy-schools-how-new-york-plans-protect-your-childs-personal-information/2571160002/.

Zimmerman, A. (2019, April 2). "New York officials report glitches with computer-based state tests, renewing concerns about Questar." Chalkbeat.org. Retrieved from: https://www.chalkbeat.org/posts/ny/2019/04/02/new-york-state-test-problems-questar.

References for Problematic School Exams—Skeptics

"Epic fail of last week's state testing; Parents demand commissioner's removal." (2018, April 17). Nycpublicschoolparents.blogspot. Retrieved from: https://nycpublicschoolparents.blogspot.com/2018/04/epic-fail-of-last-weeks-state-testing.html.

Henriques, D. B., & Steinberg, J. (2001, May 20). "Right answer, wrong score: Test flaws take toll." *New York Times.* Retrieved from: https://www.nytimes.com/2001/05/20/business/right-answer-wrong-score-test-flaws-take-toll.html.

Herold, B. (2014, January 22). "Danger posed by student-data breaches prompts action." *Education Week.* Retrieved from: https://www.edweek.org/ew/articles/2014/01/22/18dataharm_ep.h33.html.

Hildebrand, J. (2019, April 4). "Digital ELA tests to be given through April 12." *Newsday.* Retrieved from: https://www.newsday.com/long-island/education/state-tests-ela-computer-based-cbt-1.29389357.

Jacobs, J. (2019, April 17). "A testing debacle in New York may foreshadow a national trend." Progressive.org. Retrieved from: https://progressive.org/public-school-shakedown/testing-debacle-in-new-york-national-trend-jacobs-190417.

MORE: United Federation of Teachers. (2018, April 17). "Commissioner Elia and the Board of Regents continue to fail New York's children." Morecaucusnyc.org. Retrieved from: https://morecaucusnyc.org/2018/04/17/commissioner-elia-and-the-board-of-regents-continue-to-fail-new-yorks-children-parents-demand-the-immediate-removal-of-commissioner-elia.

NYC Opt Out Parent Coalition. (2019). "10 Reasons to boycott the NY state exams." Optoutnyc.com. Retrieved from: https://www.optoutnyc.com/10-reasons.

Parent Coalition for Student Privacy. (2019). Studentprivacymatters.org. Retrieved from: https://www.studentprivacymatters.org/about-us/.

Pitcan, M. (2016, June 12). "Real life harms of student data: Moving beyond the hypothetical." Datasociety.net. Retrieved from: https://points.datasociety.net/real-life-harms-of-student-data-956a30aaff32.

Spector, J. (2018, April 11). "Computer problems 'frustrating' students taking English tests across New York." *Democrat and Chronicle*. Retrieved from: https://www.democratandchronicle.com/story/news/politics/albany/2018/04/11/computer-problems-delay-english-tests-across-new-york/507479002/.

Strauss, V. (2016, April 21). "Pearson's history of testing problems—A list." *Washington Post*. Retrieved from: https://www.washingtonpost.com/news/answer-sheet/wp/2016/04/21/pearsons-history-of-testing-problems-a-list/?utm_term=.6f92cd5c3af4.

REFERENCES FOR CHAPTER 10

References for Beginning of Chapter 10 Quotes

Brown, E. (2015, October 9). "Preschool is good for children, but it's expensive—So Utah is offering it online." *Washington Post*. Retrieved from: https://www.washingtonpost.com/local/education/preschool-is-good-for-poor-kids-but-its-expensive-so-utah-is-offering-it-online/2015/10/09/27665e52-5e1d-11e5-b38e-06883aacba64_story.html.

Utah State Board of Education. (2016). "Welcome to preschool." Author. Retrieved from: https://www.schools.utah.gov/curr/preschool.

Waterford Institute. (2018). "For parents." Author. Retrieved from: https://www.waterfordupstart.org.

Wright, B. (2016, February 16). "Preschool and kindergarten are hot topics on the Utah hill." *Standard-Examiner*. Retrieved from: https://www.standard.net/news/education/preschool-and-kindergarten-are-hot-topics-on-the-utah-hill/article_0ed9b0a5-5131-50a3-90b7-35f5bda25ca3.html.

References for Cheap Childcare —Introduction

Morin, A. (2017). *13 Things mentally strong parents don't do: Raising self-assured children and training their brains for a life of happiness, meaning, and success* . New York: William Morrow.

Pedersen, J. (2014). *The rise of the millennial parents: Parenting yesterday and today* . Lanham, MD: Rowman & Littlefield.

Suneson, G. (2018, October 8). "Wealth in America: Where are the richest and poorest states based on household income?" *USA Today* . Retrieved from: https://www.usatoday.com/story/money/economy/2018/10/08/wealth-america-household-income-richest-poorest-states/38051359.

"What kind of parent are you?—The debate over 'free-range' parenting." (2015, April 26). NPR.org. Retrieved from: https://www.npr.org/2015/04/26/402226053/what-kind-of-parent-are-you-the-debate-over-free-range-parenting.

References for Cheap Childcare—Enthusiasts

Coleman, K. (2018, April 1). "Utah's 'free-range' parenting law protects parents so kids can roam." NPR.org. Retrieved from: https://www.npr.org/2018/04/01/598630200/utah-passes-free-range-parenting-law.

De La Cruz, D. (2018, March 29). "Utah passes 'free-range' parenting law." *New York Times* . Retrieved from: https://www.nytimes.com/2018/03/29/well/family/utah-passes-free-range-parenting-law.html.

Pelletiere, N. (2018, March 27). "Utah passes 'free-range parenting' law, allowing kids to do some things without parental supervision." ABCnews.com. Retrieved from: https://abcnews.go.com/GMA/Family/utah-passes-free-range-parenting-law-allowing-kids/story?id=54020213.

Thernstrom, M. (2016, October 19). "The anti-helicopter parent's plea: Let kids play!" *New York Times*. Retrieved from: https://www.nytimes.com/2016/10/23/magazine/the-anti-helicopter-parents-plea-let-kids-play.html.

Utah Legislature. (2018). "Child neglect amendments." Le.utah.gov. Retrieved from: https://le.utah.gov/~2018/bills/static/SB0065.html.

"Why Utah now has first 'free-range' parenting law." (2018, May 6). BBC.com. Retrieved from: https://www.bbc.com/news/world-us-canada-43997862.

References for Cheap Childcare—Skeptics

Dell'Antonia, K. J. (2015, April 13). "As parents stand on principle, are 'free-range' children put at risk?" *New York Times*. Retrieved from: https://parenting.blogs.nytimes.com/2015/04/13/as-parents-stand-on-principle-are-free-range-children-put-at-risk/.

Ma-Kellams, C. (2016, April 7). "Maybe free-range students isn't the way to go." *Wall Street Journal* . Retrieved from: http://www.wsj.com/articles/maybe-free-range-students-isnt-the-way-to-go-1460070663.

References for Cheap Preschool Education—Introduction

Damschen, D. (2019). "Investor information." Retrieved from: https://treasurer.utah.gov/investor-information.

Deruy, E. (2016, January 8). "This is where your state ranks in education." *Atlantic*. Retrieved from: https://www.theatlantic.com/politics/archive/2016/01/this-is-where-your-state-ranks-in-education/458784/.

"Education rankings: Measuring how well states are educating their students." (2019). *U.S. News & World Report*. Retreived from: https://www.usnews.com/news/best-states/rankings/education.

Nadworny, E. (2017, May 24). "Preschool, a state-by-state update." NPR.org. Retrieved from: https://www.npr.org/sections/ed/2017/05/24/529558627/preschool-a-state-by-state-update.

Public Finance Division. (2019). "California's current credit ratings: Comparison of other states' general obligation bond ratings." Author. Retrieved from: https://www.treasurer.ca.gov/ratings/current.asp.

Rivera, A. (2016, June 10). "Utah once again dead last in per-student education spending." *Standard-Examiner*. Retrieved from: https://www.standard.net/news/education/utah-once-again-dead-last-in-per-student-education-spending/article_3e0f14b4-df33-529b-9c92-3d7264ff57e9.html.

Withers, M. (2017, December 19). "The disconnect in Utah's public education funding." *Salt Lake City Tribune*. Retrieved from: https://www.sltrib.com/opinion/commentary/2017/12/19/commentary-the-disconnect-in-utahs-public-education-funding.

References for Cheap Preschool Education—Enthusiasts

Utah State Board of Education. (2018). "Utah preparing students today for a rewarding tomorrow (UPSTART)." Author. Retrieved from: https://www.schools.utah.gov/curr/preschool.

Waterford Institute. (2019). "Early learning curriculum software." Author. Retrieved from: https://www.waterford.org.

Wright, B. (2016, February 16). "Preschool and kindergarten are hot topics on the Utah hill." *Standard-Examiner* . Retrieved from: https://www.standard.net/news/education/preschool-and-kindergarten-are-hot-topics-on-the-utah-hill/article_0ed9b0a5-5131-50a3-90b7-35f5bda25ca3.html.

References for Cheap Preschool Education—Skeptics

Alberty, E. (2018, September 22). "Utah offers an online preschool that boosts literacy: But some Latino families, wary of sharing information with the government, are reluctant to enroll their kids." *Salt Lake City Tribune* . Retrieved from: https://www.sltrib.com/news/2018/09/21/utah-offers-an-online.

Mader, J. (2017, November 3). "Online preschool: Does it work?" PBS.org. Retrieved from: https://www.pbs.org/newshour/education/online-programs-are-filling-a-preschool-gap-experts-warn-its-no-substitute-for-face-to-face-learning.

Mader, J. (2018, October 10). "Experts call for an end to online preschool programs." *Hechinger Report* . Retrieved from: https://hechingerreport.org/experts-call-for-an-end-to-online-preschool-programs.

REFERENCES FOR CHAPTER 11

References for Beginning of Chapter 11 Quotes

Chip Free Schools. (2012, September 16). "Tracking students with RFID chips is pretty lucrative." Chipfreeschools.com. Retrieved from: http://chipfreeschools.com/featured/tracking-students-with-rfid-chips-is-pretty-lucrative.html.

Northside Independent School District—*quoted by* DesMarais, C. (2012, October 8). "Texas school uses RFID badges to track student locations." *PC World*. Retrieved from: https://www.pcworld.com/article/2011352/texas-school-uses-rfid-badges-to-track-student-locations.html.

Ozer, N. (2010, September 1). "Don't let schools chip your kids." American Civil Liberties Union. Retrieved from: https://www.aclu.org/blog/dont-let-schools-chip-your-kids.

Scholar Chip. (2019). "Class attendance." Scholarchip.com. Retrieved from: https://www.scholarchip.com/accountability/attendance/class-attendance.

References for Improving Hurricane Evacuation — Introduction

Lees, F. P., & Mannan, S. (2012). *Lee's loss prevention in the process industries: Hazard identification, assessment, and control*. Boston: Butterworth-Heinemann.

Roess, R. P., Prassas, E. S., & McShane, W. R. (2011). *Traffic engineering*. Upper Saddle River, NJ: Pearson.

Yannis, G., & Cohen, S. (Eds.). (2016). *Traffic safety*. Hoboken, NJ: Wiley.

References for Improving Hurricane Evacuation—Enthusiasts

Holdman, J. (2019, September 2). "How Dorian evacuation SC highway lane reversals will work." *Post and Courier*. Retrieved from: https://www.postandcourier.com/hurricanewire/how-dorian-evacuation-sc-highway-lane-reversals-will-work/article_4e7c829e-cd15-11e9-b4c9-83f8276694b7.html.

"Hurricane watch extended to entire Georgia coast ahead of Dorian." (2019, September 2). WSBtv.com. Retrieved from: https://www.wsbtv.com/news/local/live-updates-trump-declares-emergency-in-georgia-ahead-of-dorian/981775965.

References for Improving Hurricane Evacuation—Skeptics

Asa, R., & Camp, K. (2019, August 30). "9 Facts about evacuations in Florida." WFTV.com. Retrieved from: https://www.wftv.com/news/local/9-facts-about-evacuation-routes-in-florida/980540651.

Dunkelberger, L., & Turner, J. (2018, March 19). "Rick Scott signs $88.7 billion Florida budget, vetoes $64 million in projects." *Orlando Weekly*. Retrieved from: https://www.orlandoweekly.com/Blogs/archives/2018/03/19/rick-scott-signs-887-billion-florida-budget-vetoes-64-million-in-projects.

Turner, J. (2017, October 26). "State rejects one-way traffic in evacuations." News4JAX.com. Retrieved from: https://www.news4jax.com/news/florida/state-rejects-one-way-traffic-in-evacuations.

Turner, J. (2019, August 30). "Florida not planning one-way traffic for Hurricane Dorian evacuees." Miami.CBSlocal.com. Retrieved from: https://miami.cbslocal.com/2019/08/30/florida-not-planning-one-way-traffic-hurricane-dorian.

References for Improving Student Monitoring —Introduction

"Asset tracking." (2019). Trackseal.com. Retrieved from: https://www.trackseal.com/products/Asset-Tracking.

"Attendance tracking." (2019). Conventionstrategy.com. Retrieved from: https://www.conventionstrategy.com/services/attendance-tracking.

References for Improving Student Monitoring—Enthusiasts

DesMarais, C. (2012, October 8). "Texas school uses RFID badges to track student locations." *PC World*. Retrieved from: https://www.pcworld.com/article/2011352/texas-school-uses-rfid-badges-to-track-student-locations.html.

Merlin, M. (2018, July 22). "Big brother or safety precaution? Easton Area to require students to use IDs with computer chips." *Morning Call*. Retrieved from: https://www.mcall.com/news/education/mc-nws-easton-schools-scholarchip-20180713-story.html.

Sterling, B. (2010, September 3). "Arphid Watch: American schoolchildren." *Wired*. Retrieved from: https://www.wired.com/2010/09/arphid-watch-american-schoolchildren.

References for Improving Student Monitoring—Skeptics

Chip Free Schools. (2013a, January 18). "Andrea Hernandez stands firm." Chipfreeschools.com. Retrieved from: http://chipfreeschools.com/featured/andrea-hernandez-stands-firm.html.

Chip Free Schools. (2013b, January 19). "School officials reject request: Kick Andrea Hernandez out of magnet school." Chipfreeschools.com. Retrieved from: http://chipfreeschools.com/featured/school-officials-reject-request-kick-andrea-hernandez-out-of-magnet-school.html.

Chip Free Schools. (2013c, January 25). "A word of thanks from the Hernandez family." Chipfreeschools.com. Retrieved from: http://chipfreeschools.com/featured/a-word-of-thanks-from-the-hernandez-family.html.

Chip Free Schools. (2013d, February 25). "Community to break silence on student surveillance badges." Chipfreeschools.com. Retrieved from: http://chipfreeschools.com/take-action/community-to-break-silence-on-student-surveillance-badges.html.

Chip Free Schools. (2013e, July 16). "Victory: San Antonio public school officials end RFID tracking program." Chipfreeschools.com. Retrieved from: https://us4.campaign-archive.com/?u=f6eb78f457b7b82887b643445&id=5772781014.

DesMarais, C. (2013, January 13). "US judge rules for Texas school district in RFID tracking case." *PC World*. Retrieved from: https://www.pcworld.com/article/2025170/radio-frequency-id-chip-case-ruling-favors-texas-school-district.html.

Goodwyn, W. (2012, December 17). "Teenager's faith at odds with locator tags in school IDs." NPR.org. Retrieved from: https://www.npr.org/2012/12/17/167277175/teenagers-faith-at-odds-with-locator-tags-in-school-ids.

Vara-Orta, F. (2012, May 26). "Students will be tracked via chips in IDs." *San Antonio Express News*. Retrieved from: https://www.mysanantonio.com/news/education/article/Students-will-be-tracked-via-chips-in-IDs-3584339.php.

Vara-Orta, F. (2013, July 15). "Student tracking system dropped." *San Antonio Express News*. Retrieved from: https://www.expressnews.com/news/education/article/Northside-nixes-student-tracking-program-4667166.php.

REFERENCES FOR CHAPTER 12

References for Beginning of Chapter 12 Quotes

Cornwell, P. (2016, August 25). "Robot babies that schools use to discourage teen pregnancy may do opposite, study finds." *Seattle Times*. Retrieved from: https://www.seattletimes.com/seattle-news/education/

robot-babies-schools-use-to-discourage-teen-pregnancy-may-do-the-opposite-study-finds.

Quinlivan, J.—*quoted by* Greenberg, Z. (2016, September 1). "A strategy backfires, increasing teen births." *New York Times.* Retrieved from: https://kristof.blogs.nytimes.com/2016/09/01/a-strategy-backfires-increasing-teen-births.

RealCare shaken baby. (2019). Realityworks.com. Retrieved from: https://www.realityworks.com/product/shaken-baby.

Samuel, L. (2016, August 25). "Infant simulators, designed to discourage teen pregnancy, actually encourage it." Statnews.com. Retrieved from: https://www.statnews.com/2016/08/25/infant-simulators-teen-pregnancy.

References for Anxiety-Eliciting Prison Visits —Introduction

Bartollas, C., Schmalleger, F., & Turner, M. G. (2019). *Juvenile delinquency* (10th ed.). New York: Pearson.

Finckenauer, J. O., & Gavin, P. W. (1999). *Scared straight: The panacea phenomenon revisited.* Prospect Heights, IL: Waveland.

References for Anxiety-Eliciting Prison Visits—Enthusiasts

Shapiro, A., et al. (2003). *Scared straight!* [DVD, original film released in 1978]. New York: New Video Group.

Shapiro, A., et al. (2008). *Scared straight: Scared straight—20 years later.* [Film]. New York: New Video Group.

References for Anxiety-Eliciting Prison Visits—Skeptics

Lilienfeld, S. O., & Arkowitz, H. (2014, November 1). "How to turn around troubled teens." *Scientific American.* Retrieved from: https://www.scientificamerican.com/article/how-to-turn-around-troubled-teens.

Petrosino, A., Turpin-Petrosino, C., Hollis-Peel, M. E., & Lavenberg, J. G. (2013, April 30). "'Scared straight' and other juvenile awareness programs for preventing juvenile delinquency." Cochrane.org. Retrieved from: https://www.cochrane.org/CD002796/BEHAV_scared-straight-and-other-juvenile-awareness-programs-for-preventing-juvenile-delinquency.

Van Brocklin, E. (2016, October 17). "'Scared straight' programs divide parents as kids see gruesome results of violence." *Guardian.* Retrieved from: https://www.theguardian.com/us-news/2016/oct/17/gun-violence-youth-prevention-scared-straight-new-york-it-starts-here.

References for Anxiety-Eliciting Robot Babies—Introduction

Greenberg, Z. (2016, September 1). "A strategy backfires, increasing teen births." *New York Times*. Retrieved from: https://kristof.blogs.nytimes.com/2016/09/01/a-strategy-backfires-increasing-teen-births.

Keyser, H. (2017, June 2). "Did you have to care for a robot baby in high school?" Deadspin.com. Retrieved from: https://adequateman.deadspin.com/did-you-have-to-care-for-a-robot-baby-in-high-school-1795770827.

Leland, J. (2019, June 14). "Bringing up robot baby, a teenage rite of passage." *New York Times*. Retrieved from: https://www.nytimes.com/2019/06/14/nyregion/realcare-baby-infant-simulator.html.

RealCare Baby 3 Infant Simulator. (2019). Realityworks.com. Retrieved from: https://www.realityworks.com/product/realcare-baby-3-infant-simulator.

References for Anxiety-Eliciting Robot Babies—Enthusiasts

Cornwell, P. (2016, August 25). "Robot babies that schools use to discourage teen pregnancy may do opposite, study finds." *Seattle Times*. Retrieved from: https://www.seattletimes.com/seattle-news/education/robot-babies-schools-use-to-discourage-teen-pregnancy-may-do-the-opposite-study-finds.

RealCare drug-affected baby. (2019). Realityworks.com. Retrieved from: https://www.realityworks.com/product/shaken-baby.

RealCare shaken baby. (2019). Realityworks.com. Retrieved from: https://www.realityworks.com/product/shaken-baby.

References for Anxiety-Eliciting Robot Babies—Skeptics

Derrett, C. (2013, June 14). "*RealCare* babies teach valuable lessons to students." Wordpress.com. Retrieved from: https://youthconnectionwaco.wordpress.com/2013/06/14/real-care-babies-teach-valuable-lessons-to-students/.

Guarino, B. (2016, August 26). "Study: Robot baby dolls don't curb teen pregnancies." *Washington Post*. Retrieved from: https://www.washingtonpost.com/news/morning-mix/wp/2016/08/26/study-robot-baby-dolls-dont-curb-teen-pregnancies-in-fact-they-may-increase-abortions.

Stump, S. (2019, March 26). "Mom has the best answer when teen asks for help with robot baby." Today.com. Retrieved from: https://www.today.com/parents/teen-fails-baby-simulator-high-school-parenting-class-t150986.

About the Author

Gerard Giordano is a professor at the University of North Florida. He has written six previous books about the questions that parents have asked about the schools. All of these books, the *Common Sense Questions* Series, have been published by Rowman & Littlefield Education.

www.ingramcontent.com/pod-product-compliance
Lightning Source LLC
Chambersburg PA
CBHW020749230426
43665CB00009B/547